WINTER SHOES IN SPRINGTIME

Beryl Boxer Smeeton in Yunnan.

WINTER SHOES IN SPRINGTIME

Beryl Smeeton

Horsdal & Schubart

Horsdal & Schubart Publishers Ltd.
Victoria, B.C., Canada

Cover photograph by Margie Mayfield, Victoria, B.C.

Photographs in the text are from the collection of Clio Smeeton, Cochrane, Alberta.

Maps from *High Endeavours* by Miles Clark, © 1991, published by Douglas & McIntyre. Reprinted by permission.

This book is set in New Baskerville Book Text.

Printed and bound in Canada by Hignell Printing Limited, Winnipeg.

Canadian Cataloguing in Publication Data

Smeeton, Beryl 1905-1979
The stars my blanket

ISBN 0-920663-39-7

1. Smeeton, Beryl 1905-1979. 2. Travelers—Biography. I. Title.
G480.S63 1995   910'.92   C95-910276-0

FOREWORD

B ERYL Smeeton's approach to life had no room for restrictions; instead, she lived by a mixture of cautious pragmatism and unbridled enthusiasm. She was a woman of many contradictions, who nonetheless stood by principles as firmly grounded as the Rocky Mountains which overlook the house she and Miles built in the wild, rolling foothills of Alberta, where they are both buried.

Beryl was born on September 21, 1905, at Tolpuddle, Dorset, into a grand Edwardian world which still reflected the golden tranquillity, stability and power that was the British Empire. Hers was the classic childhood of that period and class, of stately homes, of nannies, of listening to her mother "do her bit for the troops" by warbling "My Little Grey Home in the West". Beryl loved her Nanny more dearly than her elegant, seldom-seen, Australian mother.

Governed by the myriad rules of this girlhood, she yearned to escape. She obeyed the dictates of her class, if not her heart, by marrying as was expected of her, into the military hierarchy which was her parents' *mileu*. That marriage was the last nod she gave to convention. It did not provide the independence she craved but turned out to be an unworkable predicament which, finally, she left.

Once gone, she rarely looked back. She plunged joyfully into every adventure that offered, and by the time she was in her late 20s she had trekked alone across four continents, something which, at that time, very few men, let alone single women, were attempting. Until the mid-1960s Beryl held the world's height record for women for mountain climbing without oxygen.

Yet, much as she wanted to escape her aristocratic upbringing, it had marked her, not only in her stoic grace and courage under trying circumstances, but also in the gaiety, elegance and effervescent wit illustrated by the clothes she wore — silk shirts, scarves and pearls beneath worn demin coveralls and a rawhide waistcoat with elkhorn buttons.

In the 1930s she found a soulmate in Miles Smeeton, and together they climbed, sailed and adventured until her death in 1979. Though Miles has written about their sometimes hair-raising exploits in his own many books, *Winter Shoes in Springtime* and *The Stars My Blanket* are Beryl's story, without Miles. They echo with happiness and with the excitement of vividly experienced freedom.

Sprague Theobald
Yacht *Gryphon*
Offshore Los Angeles

CONTENTS

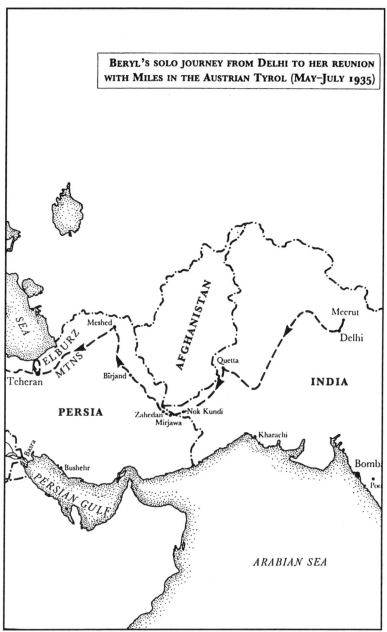

Map from HIGH ENDEAVOURS by Miles Clark.

Map from HIGH ENDEAVOURS *by Miles Clark.*

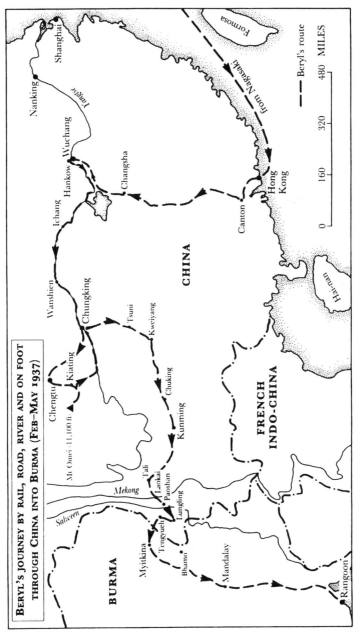

Map from HIGH ENDEAVOURS by Miles Clark.

xi

To Miles, who bought me the typewriter

INTRODUCTION

To travel is to be victorious. Never has this Arab proverb seemed more right to me than when I read the lively pages in which Beryl Smeeton recalls her original manner of visiting Asia. Her unusual will-power, fired by her desire to go her own way, conquers every kind of obstacle. Man-made regulations crumble before her determined smile; neither snowstorm nor illness, lice nor rat-bite can tarnish her bright tenacity.

Once more I am convinced that it is really people who matter most. A landscape or an idea may be of great importance, but in the end it all depends on who sees the Yangtze River, for instance, or who talks about freedom. We have been told that every human being is unique — like a leaf or blade of grass. But surely some people are more unique than others; and also when we are far from home, is it not the people we meet that matter most and help us to grasp and love a new country?

In our days of ready-made and packaged journeys, it is a rare joy to meet a born traveller. As such Beryl Smeeton succeeds where so many fail. In a strange land she makes friends at once — on board a Persian bus or when travelling steerage on a Chinese paddle-steamer. Dissolved by sympathy, the subtle poison of mistrust has no longer any reason to exist.

The first time I met Beryl Smeeton in Old Delhi, we shared a spicy curry in the bazaar, and while eating it with the tips of our fingers like the Indians around us, we compared our experiences. We strongly agreed about the importance of travelling alone in order to travel well, as light and as cheaply as possible and, of course, unarmed. One has to be accepted by the local inhabitants whenever it is possible.

"She makes friends at once": Beryl with some new friends, in Syria.

By then Beryl had married Miles Smeeton, the officer in the Indian Army whose name is mentioned in this book, and I was invited to stay with them in Quetta at the beginning of the war, when I did not know what I was going to do. In the course of the 20 years that followed, Beryl and I met in many countries. For instance, we went to Tibet together in 1945, and there I saw something of her tough side. In her presence one is ashamed to mention a blistered heel or a sprained ankle, and an illness is a detail that one keeps to oneself. What a formidable pioneer's wife she would have been in the old Wild West.

Every time we met I heard more of Beryl's past adventures, or funny stories concerning her Siamese cat, and I often wished she would find the time to write them down. At last came the winter which Beryl and Miles spent in Paris near the ·Pont de l'Alma on board their yacht *Tzu Hang*.

At that time, in spite of the visitors constantly jumping down from the quay — and always welcomed with a smile — Beryl started to type out her past journeys — there, inside the strong teak hull of the best deep-sea-going ketch afloat in her day. Poopah, the little dog, and Pwe, the Siamese cat, kept watch over the birth of that book. Now that it is completed and ready to travel across the world by itself, I would like to add a few facts which may interest readers of *Winter Shoes in Springtime*. I know that Beryl, with her dislike of personal remarks, will resent what I have to say here, and it is just as well that she is again sailing far away.

Beryl is lucky to have by her side a good partner with whom to go through life. Ever since they met they have chosen the life of youth, out of doors, a life of exertion in the mountains or the jungle or at sea. With their eyes wide open, they knew the dangers they ran and they took them in their stride. Later, after leaving the army they spent nearly ten years as hard-working settlers in British Columbia. Then they gave up their farm to take to the sea, ever ready to go to another country or to a far-away island, because it was new to them or the journey worth making.

For every sailor worth his salt, there is on this earth a piece of rock which challenges him as the North Wall of the Eiger challenges the mountaineer — a rock forever pounded by the regular heaving of the greatest of oceans. Cape Horn lured Beryl and Miles Smeeton. There, 4,000 miles east of Australia, they lived their greatest hour. Twice within eight months, they were dismasted and turned over.

Miles Smeeton has written the story of that most unusual cruise in *Once is Enough*, which is already a classic of the sea. Towards the end he makes this unforgettable remark: "and most important of all I should want Beryl if I was to take a small ship in another attempt to round Cape Horn."

He has written another book called *A Taste of the Hills* about his life in India, the Himalayas and the Alps. In those two volumes Beryl appears now and then like a figure-head going to windward, with a resolute smile, whether the way is smooth or fearful.

It seems to me that by always knowing what she wants and by realizing it, Beryl lives totally in the present moment. That rare achievement is surely a masterpiece, one of the keys to happiness. At the end of her book she describes the frightful gorges of the Mekong River. There, on a dangerous suspension bridge, she watched how an intelligent man walked slowly by the side of the caravan's leading pony, coaxing him foot by foot over the uneven boards. "It was a beautiful sight," she writes, "for I always love to see a person do something really well."

After having watched Beryl tack through 20 years of a well-planned existence, and having just left her and Miles eastward bound on board *Tzu Hang* where the clean wind is harnessed with supple sheets and sails, where the white hull leans and weighs on moving waters and where the balloon jib bulges in the brightening sun, I cannot but use her own words to describe her life: "I always love to see a person do something really well."

Ella Maillart
Geneva, 1961

CHAPTER ONE
GOOD-BYE TO INDIA

TRAVEL always acts on me like a tranquillizer, and when in 1935, seven years after my wedding day, my marriage finally broke up, a journey was what I felt I needed.

I had married young, and had moved straight from living with a widowed mother to living with a husband who was 14 years older than I was. My mother had died soon after I married, and now for the first time I found myself independent and accountable to no one. I had been living with my husband in India, and now I plunged into plans for a journey overland back to England.

Everything was going to be different. I would travel as an Indian, not as a memsahib. I would eat only native food and, I hoped, speak no English — though it did not turn out that way. I wanted to travel light, so I bought a large hold-all in which I could carry my flea-bag and my clothes, which consisted of two shirts, two sweaters, two dresses, a divided skirt, a tidy skirt, a coat, a sheepskin coat, and an evening dress. I also prepared myself by taking a few lessons in Persian and by having as many inoculations and vaccinations as I could get the doctor to give me.

I left Meerut for Quetta in May. I had decided to travel third class in a "Ladies Only" compartment. There was no reason why I should not have travelled in any other third-class carriage, but the Indian women never did, and I wanted to be as normal as possible. I was at the station early, but even then the carriage seemed to be packed to overflowing with women and babies. After some bargaining in a mixture of Hindustani and Persian I secured myself a seat not too cluttered with either babies or monkey nuts.

When at last the train left the station and we all began to settle down properly, it did not seem half so full, and I found that I could sit with my legs up fairly comfortably. All the women were friendly, and we spent the first half-hour examining each other's clothes, and I their jewellery. I had none of my own to show them and could sense that they thought me a bit queer. Banks were, after all, an English innovation and few Indians, other than businessmen, ever used them. There were none in the country districts, and as the silverfish were apt to eat paper money, the safest thing to do with it was to turn it into jewellery. This the women wore, night and day; and when they needed the money again they could always break up a necklace or sell a bangle.

There were both Hindu and Moslem women, but I could see little difference except that the Hindus were not in purdah. All the husbands, both Hindu and Moslem, were kept busy. At every station they would come rushing round to take the babies out for an airing, order food, buy water, or do some other errand that their wives had invented. However downtrodden the Indian woman may be in her own home, on a railway journey she is an absolute queen.

The train reached Sibi Junction at 11 that night. It lies at the foot of the Baluchistan hills and I could already feel that we were no longer in India proper. The platforms were full of tall, grey-eyed, arrogant tribesmen and glowing braziers criss-crossed with skewers of kabobs. The gorgeous smell of roasting mutton quite overwhelmed the stink of smoke from the engine. I bought a skewer of mutton and walked about in the fresh night air admiring the gold-embroidered waistcoats of the tribesmen. I felt quite sorry when the train started to leave.

Next morning Quetta seemed like another world. I was back again in the cantonment life that I was so longing to leave. It was as if Meerut had been lifted 5,000 feet. All the same I was quite glad to revert to one habit of Anglo-Indian life. No European in India, whether civilian or military, ever stayed in a hotel if he could help it. There always seemed to be a friend — or a friend's friend — to stay with. Quetta was no exception to this rule. Mary and Nigel Willis, whom I had last seen in Dover, were there, and I stayed with them.

I was longing to get away, but it was difficult to tell them why, for they did not know that my marriage was finished, and I could not face breaking the news to them. So it was with rather a guilty feeling of relief that I said good-bye and caught the weekly train to Nok-Kundi. In the cool Quetta air the third-class compartment seemed quite comfortable, and the "Ladies Only" was not nearly so full of children as it had been in the previous train.

This time the women were all Moslems. They all wore the *burqa*. It is a sort of coarse white cotton tent, narrowing a little towards the top, where it is gathered with elaborate stitching into a close-fitting cap. Across the eyes is a narrow little strip, three inches deep and four inches long, of lattice. It looked to me like drawn-thread work. These women's *burqas* covered them completely from head to foot. Underneath they wore anything they fancied. Unfortunately they fancied men's shirts, which pretty well obliterated their lovely saris, or, in the case of two teen-aged girls, full Spanish-looking skirts. These collarless shirts made their beautiful jewellery seem very out of place. I hoped that they were merely wearing them as protection against the dust.

Nobody seemed to bother so much about purdah on a journey. I noticed that women without husbands kept their purdah veils back even at the stations, while those with husbands lowered theirs only when they thought that the husbands were likely to appear.

Nok-Kundi was almost at sea-level, and as the train descended, the heat became oppressive; there were no fans. I was glad to see that I was not the only one who suffered; the others had equipped themselves with palm-leaf fans and were using them all the time. One of the women lent me hers for a while; I am not sure if it really made me cooler or if I was just relieved at having something to do, but I certainly felt more comfortable while I was waving it. The train kept stopping, and when it was stopped, the heat was really appalling. It invaded the carriage. We all stopped trying to talk and just sat and suffered until the train started off and the wind blew the worst of the heat away again.

At one of the halts a man whom I had seen at several of the other stops came up to the window and spoke to me in English.

"Where are you going?" he asked in a strong American accent.

"To England — overland."

"But won't you find the journey very uncomfortable?" he asked.

"Oh, I don't mind that, so long as I can meet the people of the country and live as they do," I said. "I love travelling."

"Do please come and meet my wife," he said, laughing. "You are just the person for her; she is dreading going back to Persia."

So out I got and we walked along to their second-class compartment. It was a coupé with blinds to keep off the sun, and they had
a big tub of ice on the floor; so it was cooler than my carriage,
though the leather-covered seats were not half so well suited to the
heat as the wooden ones in the third class.

The wife, Perin, was an American who had met Mohamed when
he was working in New York. He had run away from his family in
Teheran when they told him they had decided on the girl he was
to marry and that the time had come for him to do so although he
had never seen her. He had been over in the States for five years
before he met Perin. Then, as so often seems to happen with
exiles, he had fallen in love with a girl who looked like a painting
of one of his own countrywomen. She had the lovely alabaster
complexion and oval face with masses of soft dark hair, huge dark
eyes, and the long-fingered slender hands of the ladies in the old
Persian miniatures. But she was much taller, being just the same
height as I am.

Perin and Mohamed settled down to married life in New York
just like any American couple. Meanwhile, in Persia things had
changed. Shah Reza Pahlavi had captured the throne and was
trying to westernize the country. He sent out an appeal to all
Persians working abroad, especially those in the United States and
Britain, asking them to come home and help him to remake the
country. Mohamed had been greatly moved by this idea, and Perin
at once said she would go with him, so they left New York for
Teheran. This was the first time Perin had been outside the United
States and the way of life in Persia came as a tremendous shock to
her. They had to live with Mohamed's family, who had not changed
at all since he left. There were still no modern conveniences. Perin
knew practically no Persian and the family no English, and the
culminating horror was that she was separated from Mohamed, for
she had to live in the women's side of the house with his mother and
sisters, who were still in purdah, while he stayed with the men.
Luckily, just as she was deciding she could bear it no longer,
Mohamed was given a job in India. There she was able to speak her
own language and have some privacy, and things were not quite so
strange to her. Now Mohamed's mission in India had finished, they
were returning home, and she was filled with dread.

I, on the other hand, was enthusiastic about visiting Persia, but,
of course, this did not cheer her up as much as Mohamed hoped,

for I was only passing through and I had no complications like in-laws to cope with. Still, I think I may have taken her mind off her troubles for a while. There was so much to talk about that we forgot the heat, and it was not until evening had come that I said I would have to get back to my own carriage.

While I had been away, a couple of women with children had got out. This left the rest of us with enough room to stretch out; so in spite of the dust and heat I slept very soundly. Next morning I had a pleasant and fairly thorough wash in water that had been nicely warmed by the sun, for it came from a little tank on the roof of the carriage. To complete the luxury, the lavatory floor, now that the children had gone, was reasonably clean.

It was beginning to get really hot. By 11 o'clock, when the train stopped at Nok-Kundi, the whole station seemed to be on fire. The few survivors tumbled out of the stifling train, and I went to find my friends and ask their advice about my next move. Although there was a perfectly good railway right into Persian territory, the trains went no farther than Nok-Kundi, some 80 miles short of the border. It was, I gathered, the outcome of a complicated and long-standing quarrel between the Indian and Persian governments, though I quite forget the details of each individual tit and tat. Naturally enough the Indian railways soon found that business was falling off, but their government would not relent. Instead, they offered the Persians an alternative *bonne bouche* by allowing Persian merchandise to come in duty-free, provided it came in by train through Nok-Kundi and not by sea.

I therefore had to find a bus to take me the rest of the way to Mirjawa; Perin and Mohamed had too much luggage to go in a bus as they were travelling back to Persia laden with gramophones, wireless-sets, and other western gadgets. They would need a lorry to carry all this stuff. The stationmaster, who welcomed Mohamed and Perin like old friends, told them that it was too hot for the buses and lorries to run during the day, and I could well believe it. Fortunately the moon was nearly full, so they would certainly run by night. He also presented them with a bottle of a special kind of orange squash which his nephew had invented. He said it was made of pure fruit juice and was preserved without sugar or cooking, but our suspicions were aroused when he told us to be sure and drink it very quickly after we had pulled the cork.

We then took a walk round the few shops of Nok-Kundi. It seemed to me an attractive little village, but then I was in a mood to like everything. I doubt if the inhabitants, whose only water supply is brought to them on the weeky train, were so enthusiastic. We were followed everywhere we went by the lorry drivers who had realized that my friends would be valuable passengers, and there was a good deal of bargaining about the journey to Mirjawa.

When we had exhausted the amenities of the village and bought some boxes of matches to give point to our walk, we went back to the station and tried to sleep in the train. I lay for a while thinking I should never get cool enough to sleep. Then I broke out into a heavy sweat and dropped off. Perin woke me a few hours later and told me that the stationmaster had arranged some food for us. The meal consisted of boiled rice and fried eggplant. We watched Perin jealously while she was portioning it out, and a crowd of people gathered round to see us eat. It was excellent. Mohamed had told me the day before about a Persian milk food called *mast,* and now he asked the man who had brought our meal if he had any. The man said "No," but one of the men in the crowd stepped forward and offered us some, which his wife had dried and given him when he left home a month before. It tasted rather like sourish cream cheese and was very good sprinkled over the rice.

When the meal was over, the loading of the bus and lorries began. I had a seat reserved for me in the bus, and Perin and Mohamed had two front seats in a lorry. The lorries used to take their full load of merchandise and then tie on top of that, and all round the bonnet and engine, the luggage of any passengers who had come by train. The rest of the passengers in the bus were pilgrims on their way to Meshed.

We started off in the cool of the evening. The bus launched itself into the desert beside the disused railway line, for there was no trace of a road at all. We had not been going more than half an hour when we saw two figures gesticulating in the sand. Our driver at once accelerated, and we rushed past them at about 30 miles an hour. I asked why we did not stop, for the poor things really looked quite desperate, but I was told that they were probably just Baluchi tribesmen trying to rob the bus, so the driver would not take the risk of stopping.

All this time the pilgrims had been sorting themselves out, for there were, of course, far too many for the seats in the bus. By now they were neatly packed down and they all seemed to be trying to sleep, except for one old man who was sorely afflicted with a boil on his bottom, which I imagine he was going to Meshed to cure. It looked as though he would cure it or die in the attempt long before he got to Meshed, for there was no road at all and the desert was full of bumps which did not seem to deter the driver in the least.

Every hour and a half the pilgrims woke up, and a large, bearded man would chant a kind of litany and then everyone else would join in. It took about two minutes. I did not know if the words were different each time, but to me they all sounded more or less the same.

The moon had risen, and now we could see the mountains standing grimly against the sky. The moonlight made the bus cast a black shadow on the sand. There was nothing else to be seen, not a stick of vegetation, but just mountains and rocks rising gaunt and bare.

At some time in the small hours the driver stopped and announced that he was going to have a sleep. All the passengers except me and the old man with the boil were already asleep, curled up in little balls. I at once got out of my cramped seat and lay down on the sand; the old man followed suit, thankful at last to be able to lie on his stomach. The driver warned me in a rather half-hearted fashion about snakes, and then, feeling he had done his duty, promptly fell asleep. Although I was wearing nothing but a divided skirt with a thin shirt, I was soon asleep. I was annoyed to be woken up two hours later and told that we were moving on. I crammed myself into my seat, which seemed to have shrunk during the night; no doubt the pilgrims had been shunting a bit while I was away. Fortunately we would be stopped in a couple of hours' time at the gate with which India marked the frontier with Persia.

When at last we reached this gate, it looked as if it had been dumped at random in the middle of the desert. It stood in a depression which might possibly have been a river if there had been any water, and it consisted merely of two upright posts with a stick laid between them. There was plenty of room for the traffic to pass all round it, or indeed anywhere but through it. Moreover, it was not even the real frontier, for in the early morning light we could see the Persian frontier post at the railway station a couple of miles away. The gate bolstered up its prestige with a small blockhouse nearby and some guards with rifles. They stopped the bus and took our passports. While we were waiting for them to be returned, the lorry arrived with Perin and Mohamed. The passport man surprised me by asking if Perin was a permanent or temporary wife. Mohamed explained that Moslems often took a temporary wife when they were going on a journey. These temporary wives could be hired through an agency and were usually selected by the permanent wife.

There was one of those inexplicable frontier waits which lasted for two hours, during which we made some sort of a meal. We did not do too badly. I found I still had two curry puffs left, and Perin produced some hard-boiled eggs; we also had some tepid water to drink, for even in the thermos it had got quite hot.

At last, with great ceremony, the top stick was lifted off the other two and we were permitted to drive through into no-man's-land. It was not long before we arrived at the real frontier, where the Customs people took their work much more seriously. The lorry had hardly come to a halt before half a dozen men were climbing on top of it, throwing down the packing cases, bursting them open and strewing their contents all over the yard. The chief Customs official, perhaps to compensate for the zeal of his men, asked the three of us to come round to his house while all this was going on and to have lunch with him. He said that by the time the examination was over it would be too hot for the cars to go on without risking the heat bursting the tyres.

Perin and I started to make ourselves at home by washing at the tap in the courtyard when the Customs man's wife appeared and offered us a bath. We were taken into a small room and seated on two hard chairs, although the floor — and for that matter the walls — was covered with comfortable rugs. The Customs officer and his wife brought us relays of cups of milkless tea, sherbet, sweet biscuits and toffees while his wife heated the water for the bath. At last it was ready and we could wash away all the dust of the journey.

Then we went back to more tea and eventually lunch. Now that we had been joined by Mohamed and an officer in the Persian Army, our hostess had a rather difficult time keeping herself hidden in her *chador* and had only one hand to carry in the food. The *chador* is the Persian version of the *burqa*. Those worn out-of-doors are always black. Her indoor one was made of a long piece of gaily patterned cotton cloth. Ordinarily it hung round her shoulders, but when men were present she pulled it forward over her head, keeping it in place by gripping it with her teeth or holding it with one hand.

Our host kept telling us of all the luxuries he would have given us if only they had been obtainable in this little frontier town. He was full of apologies for giving us such a poor meal. We all thought it was delicious, and I do not think this was only because we were very hungry, for all the time I was in Persia I never had a bad meal.

CHAPTER TWO
A SURFEIT OF NIGHTINGALES

WHEN the army officer learnt that we were trying to make Zahedan that night, he at once offered to take us in his car, for he was returning to his regiment which was stationed there. The luggage would have to go on in the original lorry. As usual we would be driving in the cool of the evening, so there was still some time to wait, which we did in an old bungalow built by the British for railway officials. When I failed to find a lavatory in the bathroom, Mohamed called the chowkidar who led me out across the ruined garden to a small and evil-smelling shed. He blithely led the way in and showed me the exact corner which I was supposed to use. I had never seen a Persian lavatory before and was astonished because there did not seem to be any hole in the floor. I assumed this must be the usual Persian custom and was badly caught out at the next one I came to when it happened to be dark. My foot slipped into the hole and, not liking to support myself with my hands on the filthy edge of the hole, I was stuck balancing on the other foot and yelling for help. Perin came to the rescue and consoled me by saying that in Persia such accidents were supposed to bring good luck. Perhaps it did, but all the same I was not anxious to repeat the experience, and I never entirely fathomed how the sanitation was supposed to work.

Back in the bungalow I found that the *chowkidar* had provided one *charpoy* — a wooden bed with a string mattress — for the three of us. However, we managed to sort ourselves out somehow and have a good rest. Then we went to meet the army officer. We found him in the Customs house with his boots off and praying at a great rate. To my surprise Mohamed at once started to talk to him, whereupon he sat back on his heels and answered happily enough. Then he bowed again and went back to his endless prayers, sitting up between bouts to talk to Mohamed. I asked whether it was usual to pray so much and with so many interruptions. Mohamed explained that when Moslems were making a journey they were allowed to say all their five sets of daily prayers before they set out instead of at the prescribed hours during the day. The officer was getting through two days' prayers in one lump and talking to Mohamed between each prayer to make it quite clear that they were all really separate.

When at last he had finished, we said good-bye to the Customs man and climbed into the officer's old open Wolseley. It was much more comfortable than the bus. The officer was delighted at having someone to talk to, and he insisted on slowing down whenever the car passed any military post, however small, so that the men would have to turn out and salute him and we would be duly impressed. He explained at great length how safe I should be in Persia when I came to travel alone, for all these posts were especially to protect the traveller. At one of the outposts I noticed that a very odd-looking figure turned out with the other soldiers. He was dressed exactly like an ordinary Baluchi tribesman, except that he wore a soldier's cap and bandolier. The officer told me he was a Baluchi in the process of being tamed.

It was fascinating to hear about the Persian method of coping with the Baluchis. Persia is very under-populated and most of the land has formerly been much more fertile than it is now. The government wanted to resettle these tribesmen on the land and get them to redevelop it — to say nothing of stopping them from raiding the buses and lorries. Usually the Baluchis take what they want, destroy the rest, and retire into the hills, where there is no water except in a few well-concealed springs known only to the Baluchis, so no one else can live there. The Persians were also very keen to entice into the army any Baluchis who had quarrelled with their tribes or families so that they could show patrols the way to the springs and the paths through the hills. It was fairly easy to induce Baluchis to enlist, but almost impossible to prevent them from deserting, for they were quite unaccustomed to discipline of any sort and had to be treated just like shy and timid wild animals. To begin with, they merely lived with the soldiers, then they were made to wear a military belt. After a few months they were put into a military hat, and so on until by the end of the year they were fully dressed soldiers. It is very ticklish and rather disheartening work, for once a Baluchi chooses to take to the hills he can rarely be found again.

The Baluchis have very strict codes of honour, and some tribes will never attack a caravan with women in it. As a result, some women banded together and hired themselves out as safe-conducts to travellers. This came as a very welcome relief in middle age to some who could no longer hire themselves out for anything else.

While all this was being explained to me, the old Wolseley was covering the ground at a fair pace, and we were congratulating ourselves that we should be in Zahedan by eight o'clock that evening, when suddenly we were caught in a rainstorm. The driver was the only one with a mackintosh, but before we could worry about getting wet, the car sputtered and stopped. Apparently it just could not cope with rain, so we had to pile out of the car and drape ourselves and our one mackintosh over the bonnet to keep the engine warm and dry until the shower was over, when the engine started up again as though nothing had happened.

In spite of all this I was glad of the rain. In the desert under a powerful sun you cannot see much, and even when it was low on the horizon there was a glaring haze of dust. But now that the rain had laid the dust, it made an astounding difference to the view. I saw that we were going along a desert plain with mountains in the distance, all the most remarkable shapes as if a lot of cathedrals had been thrown together at random. The landscape was made of bare sand and stone; there was not a scrap of vegetation anywhere. The sunset that night was magnificent; a dark cloud lay behind the mountains and threw them into strong relief. The moon was just rising as we bumped our way into Zahedan.

All through the journey the officer had been pressing us to stay in the officers' mess, where he lived with four others. Mohamed was loath to accept for fear of offending the man with whom he had stayed in Zahedan the last time he had been there and who would certainly expect him to do so this time. But the officer was so pressing and the hour so late that we decided to go to the mess. As we had an army officer on board we were able to drive straight past the police post with none of the usual red tape. We stopped outside a green door let into the high mud wall beside a narrow road. This was the officers' mess.

We went through a mud passage, the thickness of the wall, into a fairly large oblong yard with a well in one corner and rooms opening off two sides. Behind the well was the kitchen. Only two of the officers were still up, but they welcomed us with that Persian hospitality which always amazed me. Then they hurried off to wake the other two and turn them out of their bedroom so that we could have it. These displaced officers did not seem in the least put out when they came smiling to meet us a few minutes later. A servant brought tea and *arak*, a spirit made from raisins and drunk neat, for no Persian would think of mixing water with it. Our host said that as he was so strict about his prayers he could be lax about drink, and I found that most of the Moslems in Persia were much more lax than those in India. Although it was nearly midnight, the officers bustled about arranging a meal and a bedroom for the three of us to share. Perin and Mohamed each had a camp bed and I had my sleeping-bag, so we needed no furniture.

When I returned to the yard after a rather ineffectual toilet, which I thought would pass muster as there was no competition but Perin, who was similarly handicapped, and no light but candles, I was delighted to be received by the officers all leaping to their feet and waving their *arak* glasses with cries of *"Salamati!"* I duly replied *"Nushijan!"*, as I had been taught to do. Then the servants came in with huge dishes of kabobs, a large dish of rice, and six or seven other smaller dishes with different colours and smells. None of them were like anything I had tasted in India. My favourite was *khormehsabzi*. It was made by frying equal quantities of finely chopped spinach, onions and parsley in oil until it was golden brown, and then putting it in a stewpan with a little butter and simmering it in its own juice for two or three hours; about half an hour before serving, some small chopped pieces of meat were added. The great merit of this — and of most other Persian dishes — was that the longer they were cooked the better they were, and as there was no fixed time for any meal, you could almost always be sure of getting a good one.

In Persia it was etiquette for the hosts and guests to wait until the principal guest had helped himself, then everyone else fell to. For the first ten minutes of any meal there was no conversation except people recommending the various dishes to each other.

When we reached the fruit stage the conversation became more general. It was mostly in Persian, but I was glad to find that the lessons I had taken in India were a help and that I could understand a fair amount. Many of the better-off Persians knew French, two of the officers spoke it no worse — and no better — than I did, and there was always Mohamed to translate when we got stuck. The officers were astonished to find that I was actually travelling alone and had only met Perin and Mohamed for the first time on the train to Nok-Kundi.

"What a brave young woman you are!" said one. "Aren't you afraid to travel quite alone?"

Before I could reply, our host chipped in with a cliché that I was to hear wherever I went. "In Persia," he said, "she is quite safe since Shah Reza Pahlavi rules. Now a virgin with a bag of gold can travel from end to end of the country and both remain untouched."

There was an awkward silence as the same thought flashed across all our minds: I possessed neither of these qualifications. One of the officers tactfully came to the rescue by putting on the gramophone with records of Persian songs, which I found much easier than Indian music to understand. Conversation picked up again. I was surprised to learn that our host was still only a second lieutenant after 25 years' service.

"Why?" asked Mohamed.

"He's too stupid to get promoted," replied one of the other officers.

The second lieutenant seemed no more abashed by this remark than he was by his low rank. He took advantage of the few opportunities his position offered, and he loved to display his authority to anyone junior to him.

Next morning we were woken by the sound of a flute and were called out to come and see the soldiers going on manoeuvres. We stood in the doorway watching them marching down the street two by two, with a solitary flute-player who never stopped playing as he marched beside them with an oddly gay kind of goose-step.

We breakfasted on *mast*, lovely bread from an extraordinary flat loaf about a yard long which had been brought back hot from the baker's oven draped over the servant's arm like a mackintosh, and, of course, tea. Then we decided to try and find a bath. A servant told us that there was one just across the street, so we set off in pyjamas and dressing-gowns, carrying our clothes with us. Mohamed was particularly conspicuous in a gaudy dressing-gown of his wife's choosing, and I flapped slowly along in a pair of heelless bedroom slippers. To our dismay, but to the delight of all the onlookers, the bath proved to be a good quarter of a mile away. Naturally the news of our coming reached the bath-house before we did. The owner was out in the street ready to meet us with an attendant boy and glasses of tea. After we had each been offered a pull at the water-pipe he was smoking, we got down to business and bargained for our baths.

Every self-respecting Persian village has a bath-house. Usually it consists of several sets of rooms. Each set has a room for undressing, in which there is a slab for massage, and a hot, damp room with a shower, a bath, and hot and cold water. The only drawback is that the bath-houses always teem with cockroaches.

When we returned to the mess, we found a lovely Arab horse waiting outside the door. Our host had ordered it for us, and as Mohamed was busy and Perin did not ride, I had the horse to myself. The saddle came up high in front and behind, and the stirrups had toe-caps to put your feet into, so it was really very comfortable. I started to practise riding up and down the street. I got the horse into a trot fairly easily, but no amount of kicking would make it canter until the groom called out "*Zud!*" (Persian for "quickly"). The horse immediately broke into a canter, and now I thought I would be all right on my own.

Zahedan was only a very small place, with nothing to stamp it as a real town except a couple of banks. Only in one street were there any shops. The others were just corridors between unbroken, windowless mud walls, for the windows never opened onto the street and you could see nothing of the gardens within except the occasional top of a tree growing out of a courtyard. I soon exhausted the sights of the town and rode out to enjoy myself cantering over the desert. I wished I had been born a few years earlier and that I could have ridden a horse like this along the pilgrims' road to Meshed.

Back at the mess I found poor Mohamed much upset and in an awkward dilemma. His host of the previous visit had turned up and asked why he had not come to him this time. Had he been uncomfortable there?

"Oh, no, not at all," Mohamed protested, but his friend remained unconvinced and did not seem placated until Mohamed remarked that he had so much to do in Zahedan that he might have to spend another night there.

"Then you must come and stay with me," said his former host more cheerfully.

But just then his present host arrived, also very upset.

"What will people think of military hospitality?" he demanded. "If you leave the mess, everyone will say that we have not made you comfortable. No, you can't possibly go."

It looked as if poor Mohamed would be torn in two. He temporized and asked me to come into the town with him.

"Things are even more difficult," he told me as soon as we were out of earshot of the mess. "My firm has telegraphed to say I should stay a few more days in Zahedan as they have work for me here. What shall I do?"

I knew absolutely nothing about Persian etiquette, so I could not help him at all. In the end we went to the telegraph office, and he wired to his firm that it was impossible for him to stay. On our way back to the mess we met his former host, and I wondered how Mohamed would soothe his wounded feelings. He did so brilliantly by asking him if he would be so kind as to supply us with food for the journey to Meshed, delicately hinting that he did not think much of the food at the mess. His friend was overjoyed and suggested conspiratorially that he should send the food basket ahead to the Customs gate so that the officers at the mess would not know anything about it.

At half-past five a large Buick tourer arrived. Mohamed and Perin had ordered it for themselves and their luggage. They insisted on my coming with them and refused to let me share the cost of the journey: they would have had to have the car anyway, and I, with my one bag, did not really make much difference. I was very glad to go with them. Not only did it save me money but they were great fun to be with, and I knew with them I was far more likely to see some of the real Persia.

We had a panic start, for the car had not arrived until half-past five and at six the first part of the road through the mountains was closed for the night because it was supposed to be unsafe after dark owing to raiding Baluchis. The Sikh driver did not make it any easier. He had just come a long drive and complained that he was sleepy, so that at one time it looked as if we would never get our luggage loaded in time. But somehow we stuffed it all in, said rather hurried good-byes, and arrived at the Customs gate at five minutes to six. There we picked up our basket of food, and the customs men let us out onto the mountain road without making any difficulties.

It was a fairly good road. As we approached the mountains we came across huge flocks of sheep and goats, and saw the Baluchis' hair-tents on either side of the road. Every now and then we passed small outposts of soldiers. The road led through the mountains along a valley, and most of the time we seemed to be driving along a dried-up river-bed. It looked as if a shower of rain would have closed the road. The valley was very beautiful in the evening light; all the mountains were the colours of a sunset — orange, green and purple. I lay on my back on the luggage and put my head out of the window to admire the view. I was sorry we had to hurry through; I would have liked to have got out and had time to stare.

The moon was high as we left the river-bed and began to climb. At the rim of the high plateau we came to an outpost with a couple of companies of soldiers. In the bright moonlight it looked as if they lived in a village of beehives made of brown mud.

We stopped and went into a small tea-shop lit by a lamp in a wrought-iron cage. Inside a samovar was bubbling; the walls and floor were covered with rugs, as the mud benches had been outside. We drank tea, though I would have preferred to settle down to wine and a story-teller. But Perin and Mohamed were anxious to get on. She unpacked a bowl, and he got the proprietor to fill it with fresh *mast*. Then we drove on.

The moonlight was so bright we drove without headlights, and in the clear air the moon looked utterly different from in India. Its light made the huge, bare plateau, without a living soul, look quite lovely.

We slept that night on the plateau under the moon. Poor Perin spent three miserable hours being tortured by mosquitoes. Luckily, I am impervious to most things that bite, so I just lay down on the ground and slept. At dawn we set off again, reaching Birjand in the middle of the morning.

Here Mohamed was taking no risks of offending would-be hosts, so he drove straight to the old caravanserai. These caravanserais, which the Persians for some reason called garages, were the nearest things to hotels in the smaller towns and villages. Only in the larger towns in Persia were there real hotels, and they were very expensive. The garages catered for everybody. You had the choice of a room with iron or brass bedsteads with clean sheets; an empty room with rugs; a wooden bed on a verandah or in the courtyard with one eiderdown, or a plain wooden one without. The really poor or very mean could lie down on the ground for nothing. You ordered food by its money's worth, and I found it most convenient to be able to ask for one *rial's* worth of rice and half a *rial's* worth of kabobs.

But we were not to escape hospitality so easily. It had always been the custom in Persia that a man of position who was travelling should stay with the man in the village whose rank was nearest to his own, no matter at what time of day or night he arrived. While we were having lunch, the man with the second highest rank in the village sent a servant round to ask us to stay. Mohamed was determined not to get entangled a second time and refused.

"Then my master asks you to dinner," said the servant, undaunted.

This time Mohamed accepted.

Our host's house, like the mess in Zahedan, was reached through a gate in the street wall, and behind it was a walled garden. We were shown into a room with pleasant Persian carpets on the floor, but they were ruined by hideous European furniture, ghastly Victorian chairs covered in bad plush and festooned with woolly pompoms, and gimcrack tables carefully spread with scraps of machine-made tapestry.

We sat on the plush chairs for three and a half hours, making rather strained small talk with our host, who spoke nothing but Persian, and a few friends who dropped in from time to time. Fortunately some of the friends spoke French, for my Persian chiefly consisted of some ejaculations of admiration and for drinking toasts, and "I have no money," "How much?" "It's too expensive," and of course "Yes" and "No," but my gesticulations were entirely my own and seemed to meet with the greatest success.

During this time we consumed about a gallon of tea served in small glasses the size of coffee-cups. The tea alone was quite a tax on my manners for, as usual, it was served boiling hot with a teaspoon in it. I had trouble with the teaspoon, which got out of control and burnt my nose, but I knew it was not good manners for me to hold it in the other hand. Then I committed the almost unforgivable sin of refusing sugar. In Persia sugar was taxed very heavily to raise money to pay for new railways, so it is greatly prized. If you refuse sugar, it implies that you think your host is poor and you are trying to save him money. I excused myself by getting Mohamed to explain that I had given it up to fulfil a religious vow. This went down so well that I used the same excuse for the rest of my time in Persia.

All this time Perin and I had been the only women in the room, but now another appeared — if someone veiled in a *chador* can be said to appear — and announced that dinner was ready. We thankfully got up from our ghastly chairs and went out into the garden. We seemed to have gone back a thousand years. It was enchanting: there was a full moon which looked as if you could hit it with a biscuit, a fountain playing at the end of a walk lined with cypress trees, and the scent of roses everywhere. In a blue-tiled basin round the fountain, bottles of wine were cooling for dinner. The table was laid on the verandah, within an arm's reach of the bottles. We started with *arak* and hors d'oeuvres. Then came the hot dishes; each one was better than the last, and it was almost with tears that I had at last to refuse. Our host told us that his cook had come from Tabriz, which I gathered was the home of the Persian cordon bleu.

Just as we were finishing dinner, some nightingales began to sing but nobody stopped to listen to them; they were just regarded as a nuisance for disturbing our conversation. All too soon we had finished the tea and coffee with which the meal ended, and then we had to be off, for in Persia the guests leave as soon as the meal is over.

Next morning I was struggling to wash in a saucepan on the floor when I heard a bit of a commotion outside. I looked out to see two officers trying to wake Perin and Mohamed. One of them had been ordered back to Meshed and was wanting a lift. It was a recognized drawback to travelling in Persia that at any time one might be inflicted with any officer who wanted a change of scenery. We succumbed with what grace we could and said we would love to have him, although I was already amazed how four of us and the luggage had got into the car.

When this had all been settled, another messenger arrived. It was another invitation but from a much more important man. Before the new regime in Persia, the country had been quite feudal, each district being more or less owned by a local lord, who was usually very tyrannical and corrupt. There was one exception, a man who took the greatest interest in his peasantry and gave large sums towards educating them; as a result he was much loved and trusted by his people. When the new Shah reformed his feudal system, all the bad men were in various ways deprived of their land and their powers, but the one exception was left. It was this good man who had asked us to lunch. We were thrilled to go and made what changes we could in our appearance to be equal to the occasion. Our host of the previous night even went so far as to shave before coming round to fetch us.

At the great man's house, we were shown into a room even larger and with more hideous furniture than we had seen the night before. Instead of carpets on the walls, there were oleographs of the Shah. Here we waited until the door was ceremoniously opened by two servants and through it came an exceedingly handsome, patrician-looking figure. He was tall, slim and silver-haired, with charming manners. Best of all, he spoke fluent French with an excellent accent. We all sat and talked while tea and coffee were handed round.

After a bit I asked if I could see the garden. Our host led the way out, and we found that, apart from being larger, it was exactly the same as the one where we had dined the night before. I was reminded of the nightingales and asked him about them. He laughed and, pointing to a house high up on one of the surrounding hills, said "Next month we move up there for six weeks. If we stayed down here the nightingales would not let us sleep at all."

A servant announced lunch, and we went back into the house by another entrance to find ourselves confronted with an enormous table loaded down with enough food for 30 people. The meal was in fact no different from the lunch served on any other day; what wasn't eaten was given to the poor of the village, who came each day to fetch it. The table had been laid in the traditional symmetrical style, which meant that everybody could fend for himself without stretching. I did good justice to the lovely food. I particularly enjoyed the Arabian Nights' dish of "lamb stewed to rags";

then there were the marvellous dishes of vegetables, all fried and then stewed in fat for hours, and the bowls of perfect rice. It was much better than the Indian rice which seemed almost sticky in comparison. It takes much longer to prepare and is far more bother, but to the guest it seems well worth the extra trouble. Sometimes they cooked it with broad beans, which turned it a delightful pale green, but my favourite was a kind of crust of rice which is served separately. It is really the scrapings from the bottom of the dish the rice was cooked in. The only thing I can liken it to is the crackling on pork.

In front of each guest was a small plate of raw herbs which you could add to your food or eat separately. Then there were a great many cucumbers, always served on the same plate as the fruit — oranges, apricots, peaches and strawberries. For sweets, which are not often served, we had various forms of milk and sugar mixtures, quite like Indian sweets.

After this stupendous meal we staggered back into the room with the plush chairs, and there we had more tea and coffee before saying good-bye.

CHAPTER THREE
RENDEZVOUS IN A DROSHKY

B ACK at the caravanserai we found the officer had loaded up the car and was panting to be off. So we crammed ourselves in and started for Meshed. We found him so appallingly conceited and impatient that a few hours of his company were more than enough for us. We began to look out for somewhere to stop, if only to annoy him. But though it was cold in the car and we were longing to warm ourselves, everyone seemed dead asleep in the little village we were passing. Then suddenly we saw a light and there was a little tea-house. It had three gothic windows at the end, and in the middle a wrought-iron lamp. It really felt more like a church than a tea-shop — and not only because of the shape of the windows. It all had such a lovely calm and peaceful air. At the end of the nave was a samovar boiling, and there were rugs on the walls and floors and on the benches of a little alcove outside; the full moon was shining through the three windows at the end. As I stood looking at it, enraptured, our officious passenger came rushing in, flashed his torch onto the rugs and shouted, "*Ce n'est pas propre.*" I was furious with him.

We had some glasses of tea, but the wretched officer spoilt everything by nagging at Mohamed, urging that we should drive straight on to Meshed. This did not appeal to us, still less to the driver, so we drove on again for another two hours, and then we insisted on stopping in a pretty little village called Turbat. The garage was full up inside, but eventually we found enough space on a verandah for the camp beds, and there we slept.

Next morning I was woken by the officer getting up long before it was light. It did not take him long, as he had only removed his boots and coat the night before. He came and gazed at all of us in turn, but we were relentless and all determinedly slept on. Not until half-past six did we condescend to wake up. The poor man was already pretty desperate, but I delayed matters still more by enjoying my breakfast so much that I refused to start until I had finished all the supplies in the garage. The meal consisted merely of bread and butter and honey; but the bread, unlike the usual Persian large oblong pancake apparently made with brown flour, was as crisp as a biscuit. The butter was made of *mast* and very soft and creamy, the honey cloudy and runny.

When at last I finished eating and set off in the car, the officer was in quite a frenzy. But we were less and less sympathetic. During the drive of the night before we had discovered that his chief reason for rushing back to Meshed was that he had left his very-newly-wedded wife there, and we could not take his remarks about "duty calling" seriously any more. In fact, we all hoped that if we delayed the journey long enough his wife would be in the arms of another man by the time he got back. We were beginning to dislike him heartily for being so officious and so conceited. His conceit was astounding. He talked incessantly about *"les dames"*. He told me he had been at the French Military Academy and that, when he left, all *"les dames"* in Paris were sad. He told me with an infuriating smirk that when he left the French family with whom he had boarded, "the daughters of the house, the servants, mother, father, sons, nephews and sisters were all weeping that I leave."

"Will your wife be surprised to see you?" I asked.

"Oh, yes. It will be a lovely surprise for her because she is so extraordinarily fond of me."

In spite of our tedious companion I was enjoying the journey. Even for a Christian there is a great thrill in approaching Meshed because nearly all the travellers you meet on the way are going on a pilgrimage or returning from one. Everywhere there are shrines, beggars, and a sense of excitement. As we started up a winding rocky road the driver told us that over the rise we should get our first view of the shrine. All the pilgrims put stones or coins at the spot where they first saw the golden dome of Meshed. Our first sight of it was lovely; the city looked so calm and green lying in the hollow of the arid mountains; just a clump of cypress trees and sunlight catching the gilding of the mosques. When we arrived in the city it was very disappointing. I had never been to Russia, but it struck me as just what I imagined a typical Russian town to be like from what I had read in Russian novels. The streets were rather broad and straight with huge cobbles. The houses on either side were rather uninteresting, but the droshkies which one saw everywhere were more exciting and gave the place a real Russian flavour.

We drove to an hotel which was owned by Persians and run by Russians, for the refugees from the revolution had poured into Persia and only the wealthier ones had been able to leave. The rest settled down and did not seem to be unduly discriminated against by the Persians. The first thing we discovered about the hotel was that the bath was out of order and likely to remain so for the rest of our stay. However, the public baths were near and excellent.

I had not thought I would be long in Meshed, but Mohamed had so many friends there who arranged wonderful parties for him and Perin, to which they always invited me, that in the end I stayed more than a week. Two parties were memorable.

The point of the first one was *les sports,* at which I, being English, was expected to excel. It was a big picnic on a Friday, the Moslem Sabbath. Everybody there was related to everybody else, so the women would be able to take their *chadors* off, which, I gathered, would be necessary for *les sports.* A *chador,* as I have mentioned, is a most unwieldy garment. The outdoor version is made of six or seven yards of black material, one and a half yards wide, sewn into a loop like a roller-towel. The front part is tied round the waist. The back is pulled up over the head and the *picheh.* This *picheh* is a little eyeshade made of horsehair attached to the head by elastic.

At ten o'clock in the morning the cars began to arrive. They looked as if they belonged in a comic film. There seemed to be some ten people peering out of each car, all screaming and yelling out about *les sports.* There were three cars; one of men, one of women, and one mixed. When we were all packed in, there must have been nearly 30 people, not to mention loads of foods, and quantities of children squashed into the gaps.

We got off to a bad start. Many of the roads in Persia were watered by men who use four-gallon tins to scoop the water out of the stream that runs alongside. As the leading car reached a

24

watered road, one of the road-men misjudged the car's speed and pitched a whole tinful straight into the front seat. It soused a bearded man who took such umbrage that he insisted on being taken home and refused to come to the party.

The cars stopped at some rather attractive-looking gardens a little way outside the town. Two of the men went into a garden and asked the owner if we could spend the day in it. I gathered that this was only to be expected in a country where all vegetation is private property. All was well, so we carried in the food, two samovars and lots of rugs, and we appropriated the top of the garden while the owners used the lower half. There was a little canal running through the garden where we washed and the servants could dip water for the tea. They made a fire, and when the food was ready the children brought it to the rug round which we were all sitting. The food was just as good and we were just as comfortable as if we had all been sitting in a house. After it was finished I hoped we might see something of *les sports*. But no.

"We must rest," everybody told me. "It is not good to have *les sports* directly after a heavy meal."

So we just sat there. Some people played cards, and an old man, who was the grandfather of some of the guests, smoked opium. He offered me a pipe, and I was delighted to have a chance to try it. The pipe had a small china bowl and a long wooden stem. The old man melted a small ball of opium over a charcoal brazier and stuck it on the side of the china bowl where there was a little hole. Then he handed it to me and told me to pick up a piece of charcoal with a pair of tongs and hold it about an inch away from the opium, sucking vigorously all the time. As I rarely smoke and never inhale, I made a kind of volcano in my head. As I sucked and sucked, afraid to exhale for fear of letting the pipe go out, my eyes, ears, mouth — and eventually my whole head — filled with smoke and I nearly choked. Luckily I also grew dizzy and dropped the pipe. But after a second try I got the hang of it and smoked two pipes of opium in quick succession. The old man was delighted with me and urged me to go on, but his children came and made me stop, insisting that it was a shocking habit. I was glad enough to do so as I was already beginning to have a nauseating taste in my mouth.

Now the big moment arrived, *les sports* were about to begin, and the cards and the opium pipes were put away. I was expecting something like a school or village sports day and wondered whether we should have high jumps, relay races, or putting the weight. I was soon enlightened by at least six people all speaking French at once. The first item on the athletics programme turned out to be a game of tag. Before we could start, the children under 12 were told they could not possibly play as they would be bound to ruin the game, so the poor little things were banished to the other end of the garden where they sat with their eyes popping out and watched the rest of us trying to behave like children.

The game had hardly been going ten minutes when it was stopped so that we could rest. I found that I had gained great kudos by only falling down once, while the other ladies were hardly ever on their feet. After a pause we started on the next of the sports. It was blind man's buff. A little of this and all except the most hardy souls had fallen out. People kept complimenting me on my prowess and saying, "Are you sure you feel all right? But of course you English are always so good at sports."

All the other women lay prostrate while the rest of us played Tom Tiddler's ground. When I had survived this, too, everybody agreed that only the English nation could have produced a female so sporting. (Later I heard that one of the prostrate ladies had to spend three days in bed to recover from the unaccustomed exercise.)

We were shown round the garden we had invaded. Then we complimented its owners and piled into the cars again. On the way back to Meshed we met a man driving half a dozen donkeys. Everybody at once asked me if I could ride a donkey. To keep up the sporting reputation of the English I said "Yes". Instantly orders were given, the cars stopped, the donkeys unloaded and turned round the other way. Five of us mounted them and went off for a race. It was not very fast, as the donkeys were turned away from home and reluctant to budge. But their owner beat them and the cars drove close behind them nudging their tails, so they had to go. After a mile of this foolish progress we got off our donkeys with the victor unknown and climbed back into the cars.

Two miles farther on, all the cars stopped again.

"Why are we getting out?" I asked.

"We shall take a little walk," I was told.

But nobody walked. We just hung about until we got back into our cars and started off again. This absurd ritual was repeated twice before we reached Meshed, but I never discovered the insti-gator of the idea and nobody seemed to enjoy it.

Next day Perin and I went to a carpet factory where a carpet was being made for the Shah. It was going to take four years to complete and would cost £2,000. The Shah ordered carpets from all the big carpet-making centres to stimulate the trade and revive the craft of making really fine carpets. Ministers who wanted to keep in favour with the Shah followed his example instead of importing carpets from Europe, and at this factory they were also making one for the finance minister and for a wealthy landowner.

The factory turned out to be a miserable mud-walled room with a tin roof. It was very gloomy and abominably ill-lit. There were the three carpets being made, and they would each take anything from four to seven years to complete. A different family worked at each carpet. They looked very poor, and they must have been paid very badly for there would not have been much left of the £2,000 after the silk or wool and the dyeing had been paid for and the factory owner had taken his cut. And this pittance had to keep a family of five going for four, or maybe even seven, years. Even the youngest children worked; indeed, they were kept for the parts that needed the best eyesight. The patterns were all traditional. There were scenes of hunters wearing 16th-century Persian dress and mounted on Arab horses as they pursued all sorts of different animals. I noticed one which looked more Moorish, with no figures on it, but flowers and graceful Persian writing. But in spite, or perhaps because, of the beauty of the carpets, we felt very depressed by it all and left as soon as we decently could.

There was another memorable party that night. We had been invited by the family of a man who had been a minister in the government but had "disappeared", a polite way of saying he had been killed on orders from the Shah. His family had been exiled to Meshed and all their other properties had been confiscated by the state.

The ex-minister's wife was very smart in a Paris dress. They had lived abroad for many years, and her two children, a pretty, unhappy-looking girl of about 20, and a boy three years younger, had been educated entirely in France or England. They all gathered round me, chattering away in English, while a procession of strawberries, cucumbers, nuts, tea, and Russian cakes passed slowly by. I was glad when the mother turned her attention to the other guests and I could spare time for the food. Soon the son drifted away and I was left with the girl. She was miserable in Meshed. It was such a holy place that the inhabitants were particularly bigoted and she could not put her nose outside the house without wearing a *chador*. Marriage, her only chance of escape, was denied to her for no one dared to marry into the family of a man who had "disappeared".

We went in to dinner, and afterwards we danced to a gramophone. The son, Omar, asked me for a dance and in the interval led me out into the garden. We walked out onto the grass, and when we were in the middle, well away from everybody else, he turned to me suddenly and whispered, "Will you help me to escape from here?"

"Of course," I said, and to my joy Omar at once explained his plan.

"My father had an American friend working for an oil company. He told us if we were ever in trouble to write to him. It is easy to write, but I cannot safely send the letter. Please will you take it for me and post it from England?"

"I would love to. Have you got it ready?"

"Not yet; first we will have to write it. We wanted to meet you first to see if we could trust you. Tonight my mother will write the letter. Tomorrow in the morning at about 11 o'clock, take a droshky — but by yourself, because Mohamed must not know — and drive down the main street towards the mosque. I will be walking in the street and will raise my hat to you, then you must stop the droshky and speak to me. Do not get out; I will have the note ready and will drop it on the floor."

On the way back to the hotel I found it terribly difficult to stop myself blurting all this out to Mohamed and Perin. There was good reason for keeping it secret, for it would have been dangerous for Mohamed to be mixed up in an intrigue like this. So I hugged my secret to myself and could hardly wait till 11 o'clock next morning. Luckily Perin decided to wash her hair and Mohamed, as usual, was working, so I did not have to make any excuses to go out and hail a droshky.

It was a lovely sunny day. As we trotted along the broad, ugly street, I searched the crowds on the pavements. They all seemed to be men; there was hardly one woman among them. Then to my relief I saw a hat being raised above a flashing smile, and I told the coachman to stop. Omar came up to the carriage; we shook hands and talked for a few minutes in polite non-committal phrases about the party of the night before. Then he stepped backwards and bowed good-bye. I glanced down at the floor. There was the envelope. The droshky drove on, and I did not stoop to pick up the envelope till we had turned up a side street on the way to the mosque. I felt ashamed of myself for enjoying it all so much. Omar and his family were taking a great risk — certainly of imprisonment, perhaps of death — but for me it was only a game.

I posted the letter in London. Two years later I met an Englishman who had worked in Meshed, and I asked him for news of Omar and his family.

"They managed somehow to get in touch with an American friend of his father's," he told me. "Omar escaped from Persia. I think he is now in the States and doing quite well for himself. His mother and his sister still live in the same house in Meshed."

CHAPTER FOUR

THE REGIMENT OF WOMEN

IT was now high time I left Meshed, so I asked Mohamed to come with me to the bus office to help me buy my ticket. The clerk told us the bus would leave at three o'clock the next day. When we all duly appeared at three, we found a crowd of would-be passengers sitting philosophically on their luggage while a terrific row went on in the office. A villainous-looking man, very badly marked with smallpox, was being held down by two friends while he screamed at the top of his voice and waved his arms and legs as much as he could. The office clerks, at whom his screams were apparently directed, pretended he did not exist. They talked to one another across him and around him as if he were a cloud or a butterfly. At last his two friends pulled him away, the screaming stopped, and we were able to ask what it was all about.

"Oh, he's just the bus driver," we were told. He had taken violent exception to the passengers the clerks had provided for him. Like the other bus drivers, he owned the bus he drove but left it to the clerks in the caravanserai to sell the tickets and take a commission on them.

We went off to look at the bus, and I chose a seat in the front near the driver. A Persian soldier with five women came up and started to talk to us. He gestured in a lordly way towards them and said the one with the baby was his wife. She seemed a pleasant woman but was afflicted with a dreadful cast in her eye which made it difficult to know whether she was talking to Perin or to me. They had been waiting for the bus to start since 11 o'clock that morning. Perin and I sat in the bus and watched the crowd while we waited.

After half an hour, Mohamed got fed up and went to see what had happened, for there was still no sign of the driver. The office clerks told him they had sold half the bus tickets to some pilgrims at a reduced fare, and the driver refused to start until he was paid some more money — hence the fit on the floor. And, of course, the pilgrims had no more money. After another half-hour, the driver appeared and said we would leave at once. The pilgrims meanwhile had gone off to have lunch, so they would be left behind. There were only the five women, myself and half a dozen other people in the bus when the driver started the engine. At once all the clerks rushed out of the office and made a human barrier in front of it. The driver, who was nicknamed "The Colonel" on the strength of his fluent swearing, started to throw another fit, but then he inexplicably calmed down and agreed to wait.

Almost at once a small boy ran in to say that the pilgrims had finished their lunch and were coming. The pilgrims had no sooner arrived than all the passengers already in the bus started to make a scene. I did not blame them, for I had never seen any human beings quite so dirty — let alone travelled with them. The dirtiest by far was a wretched man with seven children draped all round him. One was on his shoulder, there was one on each arm, one sitting on his hip, and two running behind. Tucked somewhere in the middle of all this was a baby, bandaged up like a mummy and looking as if it had not had its rags changed for several months. With all these children in tow he had great difficulty in getting into the bus. I started forward to help him, but the driver stopped me and in most realistic pantomime warned me I should be covered with insects if I so much as touched one of the brood. The lousy pilgrims were firmly pushed into the back of the bus, the office clerks opened their human barrier, and this time we really started.

I soon realized that I was in the right place to find out just what communal living really meant. I had bought a few packets of cigarettes hoping to ingratiate myself with the driver and his mate, but there was no need for me to offer them round; as soon as I produced the first packet, everybody helped himself. When a passenger, whom I had overlooked or who had finished his first cigarette, wanted a smoke, he would reach over and tap me on the shoulder, puffing at an imaginary cigarette. I soon discovered why I had been sent off with such enormous quantities of food. You cannot unpack your food and eat it; you must let everyone share it. You cannot take a sweet out of your bag without first pressing half a dozen sweets on each of the other passengers.

All my food, incidentally, was packed up in Persian bread exactly as if it were in cloth or greaseproof paper. The Persians wrap up food in flat bread as if it were paper. After a few hours it hardens. The food is then in a little airtight box, but once it is opened it cannot be shut again. These little parcels keep very well, and later on I went right into Russia with my Persian bread. It got a bit dirty, but it remained quite unspoilt.

At about ten o'clock that night the passengers thought it was time to stop for dinner, so we drove into the courtyard of the next caravanserai we came to. We arrived with the usual clatter and banging of a bus on a bad road, but above its noise we heard sounds of wailing and saw a crowd of about 20 people, holding lamps and candles, gathered round an old man who was lying on a heap of rugs. The bright half-moon was the only light, and as the verandah of the caravanserai was in shadow, we moved over nearer the crowd to get some moonlight. There was a woman, her face covered by her *chador* as she held the old man's hand and wailed softly. His face looked very peaceful.

We asked what had happened. They told us that he had been run over by a bus two hours earlier and that he was dying. All the passengers from our bus sat down on the moonlit ground and ordered their dinners. I joined the five women Perin and I had talked to in Meshed. They seemed to think it quite natural to be sitting and eating a good meal only five yards from a man who was dying. To me it was anything but natural, but the food was so good that I was fairly stuffing down the rice — though with slight feelings of guilt — when a sudden hush fell. Then the wailing started afresh and much louder. A new neighbour told us the man had died. I envied him and hoped that when it came my turn to die, I might do so under a moon in a castellated caravanserai — even with people guzzling rice a few yards away — and not in a hygienic, white hospital room.

After dinner we got back into the bus and drove on for the rest of the night. Some time in the early morning the water in the radiator started to boil, and when the driver got out to see what was the matter he found the fan-belt broken. He had no spare, so he searched the whole bus, including the passengers, and finally snatched a belt off a man's waist. It did not work very well and broke almost every half-hour.

We stopped for lunch at a rather pretty little tea-house opposite the ruins of a lovely old caravanserai which must have covered a good acre of ground. It had two courtyards and several halls, with masses of smaller rooms opening off them, all very tumbledown. A platoon of soldiers were living in one corner, and when they saw me taking photographs, they came out and escorted me up to the roof and posed themselves against the domes. I tried to take a photo of the little tea-house, but every time I pointed the camera in its direction the soldiers simply plastered themselves in front of it and obliterated it from view. Later I learned that it was strictly forbidden to photograph soldiers and that to use a camera at all one needed a special permit, which I had not got.

I went back to the bus and joined the five women who had been sitting on the seat behind me. We all walked to the upper part of the village where we found a stream where we could wash ourselves. I noticed that the soldier's wall-eyed wife had given up the unequal struggle of controlling her *picheh* and *chador.* She just kept one corner of the *chador* in her teeth — apparently as a mere sop to convention for it no longer covered any of her face except the bottom of her right jaw. She was travelling with her baby and now rather half-heartedly attacked the business of getting it out of its strapping and cleaning it up after its night in swaddling clothes. Every morning she took it out of its straps and left its legs free, washing the cloths in the stream and drying them on stones in the sun to be ready for the night. She then strapped it up again in clean cloths. Better-educated women only strapped their babies up at night. They have a three-cornered piece of stuff just like an ordinary English child's nappy, but several sizes larger, and they lay the baby on this with the broad side at the top and the pointed end well below its feet. Then, pressing heavily with one hand on the feet to keep the legs straight, they pull the pointed end up above the waist and strap it round with the two long ends. This is done with four or five thicknesses of cloth so that the baby is quite rigid from its shoulders down, though its arms are free. The wretched pilgrim kept his baby in this condition for the whole journey without once undoing it.

Meanwhile one of the elder women got out her hubble-bubble which she smoked on every possible occasion. I used to try too but found it was not worth the labour. I had to suck so hard and got barely any smoke and no taste at all.

By this time I had more or less succeeded in sorting these women out. The one with the hubble-bubble seemed to be of some importance, for she had two maids — a decrepit, querulous old one who seemed only capable of finding charcoal for the hubble-bubble and bringing it up every time the bus stopped, and a young, active one who did everything else. There was also a large, stout woman who seemed never to have heard of the laws of purdah. The minute she got into the bus she pushed back her *picheh,* rather as a bookie does his bowler hat on a hot day, and left it like that for the rest of the journey. She was the step-daughter of the hubble-bubble lady and was much the same age.

In some ways I was sorry that I too was not travelling in a *chador,* for it acts like a tent and makes washing and other toilet operations much easier. It is impossible to tell from behind what a Persian woman is doing under her *chador.* Not having one myself I was forced to wander off and was soon guided to the place I was looking for by the frantic noise of throat-clearings which all Persians use when there is no door.

We then went back to the bus and drove on with a break for dinner until about midnight. I must have been fairly well asleep by this time, as I only vaguely remember the bus driving into the caravanserai, and the next thing I felt was someone trying to move me. I just opened my eyes wide enough to see the driver lifting me by my head and shoulders and his mate by my feet as they carried me to the seat behind so that I could lie full length. They covered me up with a goat-skin rug and crept away. A minute later I was fast asleep again. When the driver came to wake me up four hours later, everybody except those whose seat I was occupying were already in their places. He must have been very strict with his passengers to get them all in without waking me up.

We drove on till about lunch time, when we stopped at a small tea-house. It must have been specially built for the bus passengers for it was just a tiny little mud hut in the middle of the desert with no village in sight. It was not nearly as attractive as the other tea-houses we had stopped at; there were no rugs laid about, and the building was flimsy and uninteresting.

I did not want any lunch so I waited till all the passengers had poured out, including the man with the seven children. He left the one bound baby inside the bus, where it lay covered with flies, screaming. I was feeling a bit grubby by this time and thought it would be a good idea to do up my face. As we were in the middle of a desert, there was no water so I got out my tin box with my cleansing-cream and make-up and started to work. I covered my face with the cream and left it on while I took down my hair and tried to brush some of the dust out of it. Just as I was doing it up again the bus driver saw me and, with a cry of joy, he leapt into the bus to see what I had in the box. When he saw the powder and lipstick he rushed away and came back a few minutes later with a bottle of attar of roses. He then proceeded to black my eyes and sprinkle me with scent, calling out to his mate who rapidly made up some flowers out of cigarette papers. Having decorated me to their satisfaction they led me into the room where the rest of the passengers were feeding. Here I caused great excitement, and everyone fought to have me eat with them, but I went and sat down with the five women as usual.

All this time the baby had been crying in the bus, and at last the bus driver thought he should do something about it. In Persian buses the drivers are absolute dictators. They can do anything to the passengers — kick them, beat them, knock their heads together — and the passengers, who are normally irritable, never retaliate. He now called up the father, who was struggling rather miserably with his other six children, and ordered him back to the bus to quiet the baby.

Five minutes later the driver decided we were to move on and told the passengers. Immediately a most fearful outcry began; passengers said they had been robbed and cheated, and the owner of the tea-house that he could not make a living and all the usual stuff. Once again the bus driver intervened and settled a price which seemed miraculously to satisfy everybody.

He then began cramming the people back into the bus. By this time it was so full of luggage that there was no floor space; the floor had risen to the level of the seats. The people were spread all over it, on the luggage, between the seats and on the seats. We had more or less divided ourselves into two classes, one consisting of the man with the seven children and the rest of the pilgrims — all pretty filthy — the other, the élite of the bus, of the five women, a man and a boy, the driver and his mate, and me. We all sat in front.

35

When finally we started I thought it was time I got a bit more sleep. There was some difficulty about this, as every time I dozed off, my head flopped against the window and the passengers were afraid I would break it — the window, not my head. So the driver ordered one of the passengers to give up a pillow, which I held in my arms and rested my head on. After I had been asleep in this fashion for what felt like five minutes, the woman behind woke me up to tell me that they were very sorry for my husband if I always slept so much. Then they started snapping their fingers at me, asking if I could do it too. Unfortunately it was quite beyond me, so instead I put my finger in my cheek and popped it. This had an instantaneous success; the driver took both hands off the wheel to try it, and all the passengers shouted with joy. Finally we stopped the bus to have a better demonstration. Everybody was keen to know if it was an English or an Indian speciality.

The driver's mate showed his approval by making some more paper flowers, and the man behind leant over and gave me some coloured ribbon. By the time we reached Teheran I was covered in flowers and stinking of scent, with coal-black eyelashes and eyelids.

I had been talking a good deal of Persian to the five women. I was not at all sure how much they understood me or whether I had always understood them aright, but I thought that the hubble-bubble lady had asked me to stay with her in Teheran. So when the bus stopped at an old caravanserai on the outskirts of the city I was rather slow about collecting my baggage and then took a long, tender farewell of the bus driver and his mate. All this time I was watching the five women out of the corner of my eye. To my delight I saw the elder one leave the others in charge of the baggage and come over to me. There was no doubt about what she meant this time. She took my hand in one of hers and waved the other in the direction of the city.

"My home," she said. "You come with me."

This Persian was so basic that I was sure I understood. I picked up my baggage and we joined the rest of the group.

We drove in droshkies through the modernized part of the city where the old buildings had been pulled down and the narrow streets replaced by broad thoroughfares. Then we turned off into a quiet road with a high wall along one side. We passed the British Legation and quite soon afterwards stopped at a handsome wooden door in the high wall. The old lady rang the bell and banged excitedly on the door. It was opened by a manservant who did not seem to recognize her, but he went off and came back with a woman who did. She shrieked and flung her arms round the old lady and then urged us all to come into the house. The house was lovely inside; it was a maze of rug-filled rooms and little court-yards with fountains, and there was a large garden.

By now it was late in the evening and I was ready for bed, but first we had to have a meal. We all sat on the floor and waited. I kept dozing off to sleep, being woken up every now and then to be intro-duced to a new member of the family who had been woken up to be introduced to me. At last an enormous meal appeared and was laid on a tablecloth spread on the floor. It was well worth waiting for, and we all fell on it, cramming our mouths with food and passing the different dishes back and forth across the cloth to one another. Persian hospitality consists in supplying the food. It is up to the guests to help themselves while the host sits quietly eating.

Suddenly the door opened and a very tall, good-looking man of about 35 came in. He walked straight across and spoke to me in excellent French.

"You must excuse this primitive house and lack of chairs," he said and went on to apologize for the poor meal and inadequate hospitality.

I thought that was an outrageous reflection on the old lady who had invited me, and I was most indignant, so I was very off-hand with him, especially as he went on disparaging everything else. Moreover I was very tired and found it a great strain to switch to French after two days of stumbling along in nothing but Persian. By the end of the meal I was longing for some peace and quiet.

Fortunately he noticed it, for he said, "You must be tired; I will show you to your room."

He rose to his feet and so did the old lady, and we all walked in single file through the courtyards, little rooms and passages to another tiny room. This one was furnished with a wash-stand and a European bed with clean sheets. Though I was longing to throw myself on the bed and go to sleep I thought it would be only polite to admire some beautiful roses in a vase by the bed. This was a mistake, for the man at once hauled me back into a courtyard to pick some more. But at last I was left alone and without bothering to unpack I fell on to the bed and asleep.

I seemed to have been asleep only an instant when I woke to find my room full of women. There were no less than six of them, all talking. When they saw that I was awake they all clapped their hands and laughed and smiled. They told me they had come to see if I was ill, for it was half-past eight and I was still asleep. Apparently they had been up since six-thirty, and they certainly looked very lively. They said they had a great surprise for me: there was a bath in the house and they had given orders to have the water heated.

Tea was brought, and while I was drinking it I thought I had better find out where I was.

"Who is the man who spoke French to me last night?" I asked.

"He is the owner of the house," they told me.

I was rather taken aback. The old lady with the hubble-bubble who had invited me, far from owning the house, was merely a very distant relative of the owner, who was a minister in the Shah's government. His name was Hamid.

I felt very upset about my behaviour of the night before. While I was still in bed, a young man of about 19 came in.

"My uncle has had to go to his office," he told me in excellent French, "but he has asked me to inquire if there is anything you need."

"A bath would be marvellous," I replied.

He spoke rapidly to the women in Persian and then turned to me and said, "That is already arranged. When you have finished I will go with you to the town and show you round."

As soon as he left, the nine of us who were still crowded in the tiny room — the five women from the bus, three from the house, and myself — all went to the bathroom. There was only room for six of us inside; the other three women were forced to stay on the stairs outside, peeping round the door occasionally to see what was going on inside. When it was quite clear that I was not going to be left to have my bath alone, I took off my pyjamas and turned on the shower. At once I was attacked by people with loofahs who slapped, pummelled and soaped me, and when they had given me a thorough rinse they took me aside and dried me. Then they all escorted me back to my room and watched while I dressed.

The two main rules of Persian hospitality are: Never leave your guest alone; Never let him be so bored that he wants to go to sleep. By the time I was dressed — each garment having been minutely examined by nine people before I put it on — it was time for lunch.

The meal was served in an enormous room, and we sat on chairs round a huge table. When my host arrived I tried to thank him and make amends for my rudeness of the night before: "I didn't realize it was your house. I thought it belonged to the lady from the bus..."

"But that is the way things are here in Persia if one is of the same family. It is her house while she is here."

"You have been so kind," I said. "I will not bother you any more but will find myself a hotel this afternoon."

"Oh, no, don't do that. My house is always full of women coming and going; one extra makes no difference at all."

So in the end I stayed there a fortnight, living entirely among Persians. I soon got accustomed to doing everything surrounded by a mob of people. I could not write a letter without frequent interruptions.

"How is the letter getting on?" they would ask.

And a little later: "Who are you writing to?"

I would tell them, only to be asked, "Will you send a message from me?"

And before I had written half a dozen lines, "Have you put my message in? Is it written down?"

For the first time I understood what poor Perin had been through. Admittedly I was enjoying every minute of it, but these people were not my relations and, unlike her, I could pack up and leave whenever I wanted to.

Hamid was a wonderful host. Being a minister of state he was entertained a great deal. He always took me when he went to parties given by other ministers or rich businessmen. They were much the same as those in Meshed, but they were grander and the food was, if possible, even more delicious. Although the guests were not all related, the ladies always discarded their *chadors* once they were inside the house. The Shah's attempts to abolish the *chador* were a constant topic, hotly debated at parties. As I had lived like a Persian for a few weeks I felt qualified to join in and nearly ended up by defending it; the *chador* was such a wonderfully convenient means of hiding untidy hair or unironed clothes, and it made such a handy tent when one was travelling by bus. The

Persian ladies pretended they liked it because it was so useful for love affairs, and they told lots of stories of "dangerous rendezvous" when they slipped out in a maid's *chador* to meet a waiting lover. But somehow I could not believe they were nearly as gay as they said they were.

The Persian women make no effort at all with their appearance unless they are expecting a man to see them — the men and women live in separate parts of the house and do not meet except by special arrangement. They seem to get straight out of bed and wrap their house *chador* over what they have been wearing all night. The only make-up they are never without is kohl for their eyes. I never saw a Persian woman without her eyeblack except in a bath-house. The richer women use powdered black pearls for the purpose.

For the Persian way of life the *chador* is ideal. It breeds no competitive dress-consciousness, for all *chadors* are exactly the same except for the material. The younger women, and a few well-travelled older ones, look very smart when they are dressed for a party. But their shoes and stockings usually let them down. All kinds of stockings are the same to them — they do not even seem to notice if there are ladders and holes. And their shoes are just as sloppy. I always longed to point out that an elaborate silk dress could be spoilt by cotton stockings with holes and shoes with run-down heels and broken straps. But they never asked my advice. After all, my own wardrobe was so limited that I obviously did not understand such matters.

Hamid was very good company, and I felt he really enjoyed talking to me. I gathered that he was unmarried, but as this was most unusual in Persia for a man of his age, perhaps he was a widower. He had lived for many years in France, and he said that after being so long in Europe he did not want to marry a Persian woman. He liked the independent outlook of European women and had very nearly married a Swiss girl.

"But," he said, looking round the dining-room table at ten rather blowsy women of various ages, "the life here would have been too hard and strange for her. Although I am well off now, at any moment I might lose my job."

That was the nearest he came to telling me his real opinion of the Shah.

The women in the house, including the lady who had invited me, were all poor relations, though I never worked out where the soldier's squinting wife fitted in. As soon as Hamid had become a minister, women had descended on him from all parts of the country, sped on their way by the people who had been responsible for them till then. It was taken for granted in Persia that the wealthiest member of the family looked after all the unmarried women and widows and that it was his business to find jobs for any men. As far as I could make out, the house was run by Hamid's sister, the mother of the French-speaking boy. She it was who entertained the guests, who came in hordes nearly every day, while Hamid paid not the least attention to them.

One dear old man, well over 80, came because he had heard there was an Englishwoman in the house. He addressed me in very very slow English but without a trace of an accent.

"I ... was ... last ... in ... England," he said, and paused even longer than usual, "for ... the ... Jubilee ... of ... Queen ... Victoria." I thought he was doing very well, for he had hardly spoken English at all since then. He was very anxious to know if we still waltzed in England. It seemed to be the only thing which had made a lasting impression on him. When I said "Yes", nothing would satisfy him until I had waltzed round the table, counting, "One, two, three — four, five, six," while he hummed the tune of "The Blue Danube".

CHAPTER FIVE
CASPIAN INTERLUDE

A LL this time I had been trying to get a ticket through Russia, crossing the frontier at a small town called Julfa, not far from Tabriz in the north of Persia, instead of going the usual way across the Caspian to Baku and thence by International Express.

There was an Intourist office in Teheran and I paid them a visit nearly every day. Poor things, they did not know what to say to me. They had to refer to Moscow before selling any tickets, but they did not like to admit it, so it was some time before I realized that they were only stalling when they kept saying, "All will be ready tomorrow." Finally I dragged it out of them: nothing could happen until they had an answer from Moscow. And a telegram took a week or ten days.

I went back to the house and at lunch broke it to Hamid that I still had some time to kill.

"Where can I go for a week?" I asked. "I want to see as much of Persia as I can while I am here."

"I know what you can do. Abdul, the Minister of Transport, is going to the Caspian to inspect the work on the tunnel they are building through the mountains. I will ask him to take you with him."

That evening Hamid came back and said it was all arranged and that I must be ready to start the day after tomorrow.

I was ready in plenty of time, but at half-past seven in the morning, when the car was expected, the telephone rang. Hamid answered it and came back to me in fits of laughter.

"Abdul has just telephoned; his wife only found out half an hour ago that you were going and now she insists on coming too; she will need about an hour to prepare. They will be here as soon as she is finished."

In another hour there was a great hooting at the gate and out we all trooped; Hamid and I and almost a dozen women all carrying various bundles of food. Abdul proved to be a small, round, jolly Persian. He jumped out of the car and, seizing my hands, began to apologize in voluble French for being so late. He then introduced me to his wife, who was totally concealed in a *chador*, so I had no idea what she was like.

The car was a big open tourer, and we three all sat in the back with Abdul in the middle. All the parcels from Hamid's house were carefully stowed away with the food Abdul and his wife had brought. The car was loaded to the gunwales with the stuff.

At last it was all in, and the driver started the engine.

"Good-bye, good-bye," I said to the women, some of whom burst into tears, which seemed a bit unnecessary as I was only going away for a week. Then at last we drove off.

It was all very different from the bus journey from Meshed. The car was far more comfortable and the scenery quite different. We were going to cross a range of mountains where there were trees and snow; indeed, the snow made the road impassable except to animals and people on foot for most of the year, and ours was the first car to cross since the previous summer. These heavily wooded mountains were almost the only forests in Persia and were therefore very much admired. I am no tree-lover myself — gaunt bare rocks against the sky are my preference — so I did not appreciate the forests as much as I ought to have done.

Abdul was such a jolly soul that any awkwardness that there might have been at first soon passed. His wife pushed back her *chador*, and I saw that she had a very attractive, strong, intelligent, face. She spoke no French at all, but at our first halt for food — we had one every hour and a half — I tried my Persian on her. She was delighted, and we understood each other surprisingly well. She spoke slowly with clear gestures, but it was the lively, intelligent expression on her face that helped me the most.

When we arrived at the beginning of the tunnel, Abdul and the foreman went off without us. I think that there must have been some superstition about the tunnel and it was unlucky for women to go into the tunnel while work was still in progress. So Khanum (as she was always called — it is Persian for Madame) and I sat down to have another snack. While we were eating, she told me a story about the Shah and the tunnel. The tunnel had been the Shah's own idea, and he was extremely keen to see how it was getting on. A few weeks after he had given orders for the work to begin, he paid a surprise visit to the site. In the usual dilatory Persian way nothing had been started, and the first workman he met was only an ordinary road mender.

"Where is the beginning of the tunnel?" asked the Shah.

The road mender had never heard of it.

This sent the Shah into one of his famous tempers. So his terrified staff combed the surrounding country for a man who knew something about the project. At last they found a junior engineer, but when they brought him before the Shah he collapsed in a dead faint. He had to be carried to hospital where he remained unconscious for some weeks.

While she was telling this story, Khanum's whole face was alight with excitement, but as I followed her simple Persian I found it very difficult to hide my disbelief in its ending, and I must have failed for she solemnly protested that it had been told her by an officer on the staff who had seen it all happen.

After an hour or so we saw Abdul come back, followed by a workman carrying an enormous bowl of *mast,* so we fell to and began yet another meal. When we had finished gorging ourselves, we climbed back into the car, which crept slowly upwards over a very poor road. The drive down the other side was lovely, and we kept meeting donkeys driven by peasants wearing the old national dress. The women were very attractive; they wore no *chador,* just a white cloth tied round their hair, and baggy Turkish trousers in all sorts of brilliant colours, chiefly bright pink, red and blue. Round their hips over the trousers they wore thickly pleated little ballet skirts about 18 inches deep and made of gaily patterned material. A shirt with a sleeveless bodice in a contrasting colour completed their dress, though most of them seemed to carry a shawl as well. These peasants were for me the most interesting part of the journey, as they were certainly the last human vestiges of old Persia. If I had had my own way I would have preferred to see more of Persia's antiquities and have gone to Shiraz and Isfahan, but the Persians insisted that the Caspian was much more attractive. They wanted me to see the signs of progress, the new tea industry, and the beginning of the new railway line that would eventually connect the Caspian Sea with the Persian Gulf.

Abdul was going to see these railway works and on the way there we passed some of the new tea-gardens — which to me looked pretty much the same as the ones I had seen in India. Khanum told me that the Persian tea was not nearly so good as the Indian but it was much cheaper.

"That's only because our own tea is so heavily subsidized," Abdul replied bitterly, "while the Indian tea has a big tax on it."

After a night in a sort of rest bungalow where we met some Swiss engineers who were working on a bridge, we drove on through groves of oranges — called "Portugals" because they were introduced by the Portuguese — to a dilapidated spa, once renowned for its sulphur baths.

For Khanum this was the big moment of the whole trip, and Abdul had not originally planned to visit it. Before our car had even stopped outside the huge, faded, mustard-coloured building, which in Tsarist days had been a smart hotel, she began to exclaim: "How beautiful! How smart!" When we went into a large hall with an unwashed marble floor and pillars, she turned to me saying, "How you must feel at home!"

In the old days the hotel must have housed at least 250 guests, but now there was nobody but us. If I had been alone I should have been depressed by this departed glory, but Khanum's excitement was infectious, and in no time we were all wandering eagerly in different directions, each calling across the vast, empty spaces to the others to come and look at some new wonder.

A few shabby servants smiled tolerantly at our excitement and when it had died down they showed us to our rooms. They, too, were on the same enormous scale, with huge, dubious-looking beds. In a large dining-room we had a good Persian meal, and after a long siesta we went off to try the sulphur baths.

The baths were in separate little huts outside the hotel. Abdul and Khanum were shown into one and I went into another. I did not stay long in the hot, sulphurous bath and rushed out quickly to get away from the smell. It was two hours before my friends reappeared. They were surprised to hear that I had not stayed in longer.

Khanum threw a sultry glance at her husband as she said, "If you had had a husband with you, you would not have been so quick."

That evening we ate our fill of superb caviar, and Abdul arranged to take a lot more away with us. They were surprised at my enthusiasm, for in Persia caviar was as common as lobster in England. It was ridiculously cheap and was all sold to the Soviets, who drove a hard bargain and bought the stuff dirt-cheap, only to export it from Russia at a vast profit. It was difficult for the Persians to transport the produce of their Caspian provinces over the mountains so they had to sell it to the Russians whatever the price. This was why they were so busy building railways and roads.

Khanum was so happy in the hotel that she easily persuaded Abdul to stay another day there. We went for a drive over a rough track which ran more or less parallel to the shores of the Caspian Sea. But it was misty weather so there was not much to see. Our frequent stops were dedicated to eating the caviar which we carried with us.

Abdul spent the time telling me in French about his love affairs with the girls in Paris. Khanum would watch us closely and, as soon as she and I were alone, would ask for every detail. I never could make up my mind how much to tell her, but she was a broad-minded woman so there was little I did not tell. She told me that she had been passionately keen to go on a pilgrimage to Mecca but Abdul disapproved.

"People would laugh at me," he said, "married to a Hajji."

But as the result of staying at the Caspian Hotel, and perhaps because of the stories I had told her of her husband's behaviour in Paris, she determined to go to Europe with him on his next official journey.

"What about your *chador*?" I asked.

She looked at me, raised her hands and made a vigorous gesture: "Outside Persia, *chador* pouff!" she said.

Abdul listened to this with alarm. "No, you could not come. I would not be given the money for you as well," he said.

"That does not matter; I am rich; I will pay," she replied.

She spent the whole of the journey back to Teheran in planning her European trip, and I found out that she was indeed very rich, far better off than her husband, and she seemed to have a good deal more freedom to use her own money in her own way than I should have expected from what I had seen of Moslem law in Persia.

I was really sorry when we drove back into Teheran and I realized that our journey was over. I had never thought I would enjoy it so much.

Next day I went round to the Intourist office and was received with beaming smiles. My passport with a visa for Russia, my third-class food and hotel accommodation and railway tickets were all produced one by one and handed over to me as if they were a gift of diamonds. And I was so glad to get them I received them as if they had been diamonds. Then I dashed down to the caravanserai to get a seat on a bus for Tabriz. The first one was leaving in two days' time, so I booked a seat on that and went back to Hamid's with my news.

On the morning of the day I was to leave for Tabriz, Hamid rang the bus station to make sure that I had understood the time right. I had thought it was one o'clock, but now they told him it was not leaving till four.

I had nothing particular to do and felt I needed exercise before a very sedentary journey, so I borrowed a manservant's bicycle, a formidable affair with only one handlebar, and started to bicycle up the hill to Shamran. This is a kind of hill-station where the well-to-do inhabitants of Teheran take refuge in the hot weather. Although it is only some ten kilometres away, it is much higher and certainly much cooler. As I pedalled my way grimly up, buses slowed down as they passed and people leant out to shout encouragement. Some people even stopped their cars and got out to ask me my nationality, for it was a very hot afternoon.

When I got to Shamran, I turned round and started back, but to break the monotony of the journey I decided to take a side road that looked as if it would eventually lead into another part of Teheran. I was bicycling along, my eyes fixed on the road, which was very poor, and wrestling with my one handlebar, when suddenly I found myself surrounded by barrack-like buildings and among a lot of horses. I heard some men shouting and then the road was blocked by soldiers, all looking rather alarming, armed as they were with modern rifles. I promptly fell off my bicycle and sat on it where it lay, as this seemed to be the safest way to await developments. The soldiers all started shouting and talking but much too fast for me to understand, so I said in what I thought was correct Persian, "From Shamran to Teheran." They were a little quieter after this, so I tried to remount the bicycle, but they at once became very hostile, so I sat down on the ground again. There I was stuck for a good 20 minutes until finally they got tired of my parrot-cry of *"Az Shamran dar Teheran"* and waved me on.

It turned out that all this had taken me much longer than I had planned, and when I got back I found the road to the house lined with anxious servants who thought I had been kidnapped. I told them what had happened and they were amazed that I was still free, for I had been along a military road absolutely forbidden to foreigners, and even to all Persian civilians, into the most hush-hush military area. Had I been a man, I should have most certainly been arrested.

CHAPTER SIX

A LAST FLING IN TABRIZ

WE rang up the bus station again, and this time they said they were starting at six o'clock. After many tearful farewells, Hamid, two nephews, a niece and six women, each carrying a parcel of food, all accompanied me to the caravanserai. The women told Hamid to make sure that I sat next to another lady in the bus, and Hamid duly asked the bus driver to arrange it. But, whether they thought I was a man in disguise or what it was, not one of the women passengers would come near me. So there I sat, shunned by all, until a man braver than the rest sat himself down beside me.

I was glad when the bus left at last. Hamid had been so kind to me and I did not think we would ever see each other again, so the long-drawn farewells were a miserable business. The bus drove on steadily till three in the morning when we stopped at a cara- vanserai. All the passengers got out, and they told me we were going to have three or four hours' rest.

After my previous bus ride, I thought it would be simpler for me to stay in the bus instead of going out and looking for a bed, so I spread myself out on the seat and prepared to go to sleep. I had not been there long when I felt someone pulling at my coat and feet and looked up to see the driver. He did not attempt to speak to me but made it very clear that I was to get out of the bus and follow him.

He led me out of the caravanserai and a long way up the street till we came to a notice-board which said "Otel". We went inside and a man appeared and showed me a large room with two beds.

This looked as if it might be a bit expensive, and sure enough he wanted to charge me about four shillings for only half a night, but I beat him down to about a shilling. Then I washed my face and lay down on the bed. I suppose I must have dozed off, for I was suddenly woken by a noise and I looked up to see the driver standing by my bed and wearing nothing but a string bag. I was a bit startled but tried to look as if nothing out of the ordinary had happened, and when he sat down on the edge of my bed, I yawned as loudly and obviously as I could and turned my back on him. He sat there a little longer and then went and got into the other bed.

At about six we were wakened by the "Otel" man banging at the door. I looked across the room and saw a mound of bedclothes gently heaving on the other bed, so I sprang out hastily to get my washing done as quickly as possible before the driver had a chance of making an even worse exposure of himself than the night before. But no sooner had I got the basin filled and started to wash my face than he came over and began washing his face in it too, so we had a pretty matey time — though decency on my part, and slovenliness on his, prevented us from washing any further. At last he put on his clothes, and I felt more at ease now that he had his shirt and trousers on. Then we called for a bowl of *mast* which we shared amicably enough.

When we came to pay the bill, I was astonished to find that the driver insisted on paying it all himself. Whether he thought it was the gentlemanly thing to do or whether he wanted the "Otel" man to think he had got his money's worth, I do not know.

When I got back to the bus the little man who was my neighbour asked how I had spent the night.

"Very bad," I replied. Then I pointed to the bus driver and said in loud, clear tones, "Bad man."

This was received with much head-shaking.

"You must spend the next night with me and my brother," said the little man solemnly. "He is also on the bus and we will protect you from the driver. He is no good."

Thereafter the two brothers took complete charge of me. They helped me in and out of the bus and fed me as if I was as helpless as a child or a lunatic, and when I tried to doze they made me rest my head on their shoulders. One of them insisted on giving me his rosary, though I never discovered why — perhaps it was to ward off evil bus drivers.

In the course of the day the bus developed the usual trouble — a boiling radiator — but the driver seemed to have no remedy. So for the rest of the 30 hours to Tabriz, he had to stop every quarter of an hour or 20 minutes and fill the radiator with water which he carried in spare petrol-cans, refilling them when we came to a stream or tea-shop. The two brothers who had taken charge of me spent their journey in trying to find out the story of my life. I did not think that they had understood much of what I had tried to tell them in my very primitive Persian until I heard them repeating to a total stranger everything that I had told them. This recital took a good half-hour and needed several cups of tea to help it down.

That night we stopped early at a caravanserai, no later than 11 o'clock. The brothers at once whisked me off and took a room with three wooden beds, each covered with a large counterpane called a *rezia* in India. They then ordered dinner, and after dinner they took out their opium pipes. I gained a certain distinction because I was able to smoke one without them showing me how to do so. I had a nervous moment when I saw them starting to take their trousers off, but all was well for they remained perfectly decent in long, white cotton underpants which were tied round the ankles with a tape and had a little embroidered frill falling round the feet.

Just as we were settling into our respective beds for the night, the driver appeared and tried to get me to go away with him again, but the brothers drove him off and we slept in peace.

Next morning we were all woken up by the shouts of the infuriated passengers who had apparently all been up for hours and were sitting in the bus ready to go. But we delayed matters a little more because the brothers found my camera and insisted on taking photos — none of which came out — of each other and me getting out of bed. We then called for the reckoning, and they in their turn refused to let me pay my share.

Back in the bus we went on at the same slow rate, stopping every 20 minutes to fill up with water, and we did not reach Tabriz until late in the afternoon. The brothers went out and got a porter for me and told him to take me to the house of a relation of Hamid's with whom I was going to stay. I said good-bye to them, took their address, and promised to have lunch at their house next day to meet their wives and families.

The porter and I had some trouble in finding the house, but after walking through a maze of little streets we finally arrived in a cul-de-sac with a handsome brown wooden door in the wall. I knocked, and it was opened by an exceptionally ugly but pleasant-faced maid. She gave an exclamation, of what I hoped was joy, and called out something I could not understand. In a moment the courtyard was full. The first arrival was an exact replica of the maid; she was closely followed by the lady and gentleman of the house, who made me feel really welcome and immediately began to press all sorts of food and drink on me. I had some difficulty in escaping to the public baths.

When I returned, Faiz and his wife, Shirin, asked me whether I would rather go to a cinema or to a soirée — for some friends were giving a musical soirée and we were all invited. Naturally I plumped for the soirée.

When we arrived, most of the men were already there but the women were still to come. I was introduced to the elderly host, his two brothers, and several young sons, and then I was taken into the sitting-room and given the chair of honour, plumb in the middle of the room, while French-speaking guests were led up to entertain me. Then women began arriving. It was a "relations-only" party so they could all take off their *chadors*. The hostess was the most amazingly young-looking woman for her age that I have ever seen. She had married at 14 and was now only in her 30s, though several of her sons were grown up.

We drank sherbet, tea, *arak* and beer. As usual in Persia everybody drank a great deal, which seemed odd to me after India where none of the Moslems drank. Conversation languished over the drinks until the wits of the evening arrived: a tall, stout man with a large paunch and his bun-faced wife. Everybody brightened up at once and frantically plied the new arrivals with tea, *arak* and nuts. Now, I was told in French, the fun would really start.

The three sons of the house began the musical part of the soirée. One played a violin and one a Persian drum, which is held in both hands and beaten with all four fingers while it is supported by the thumbs. The third boy had gone quite western and had made himself a one-man jazz band from two cigarette tins, a gong and a child's drum. They started off playing Persian music and then, as a compliment to me, what purported to be a fox-trot and a waltz. I could always recognize the European tunes when they began, but as they went on they became more and more Persian and less like the originals.

Someone suggested dancing. The ladies at once displayed great coyness and had to be dragged onto the floor by main force. One, who was more old-fashioned than the others and had refused even to remove her *chador,* tucked her feet under her chair and said that as she had had six children there was no need for her to dance.

After about four dances the tall, stout, paunchy man was asked to give a solo dance. He was wearing breeches and boots, with a kind of Russian blouse and a belt. His head was very nearly bald all over and he had long dewlaps, like a bloodhound's, and a long, drooping nose. With a face of great gravity he got up and went to the centre of the room and started to dance to music which by now was entirely Persian. I was amazed how gracefully he danced in spite of his heavy paunch. As he warmed to his work he began to imitate a woman and came round to each of us, waggling his behind and making soulful eyes. With his grey hair, bald head and quivering dewlaps, without a vestige of a smile on his face, he danced in turn to each of the men, delicately moving his gaitered legs. Then he danced out into the middle of the room again, waving his bottom and stamping his feet. When he tried to stop, the frantic applause drove him on till he was purple in the face and panting. He was saved from complete collapse by one of the boys suddenly leaping into the centre of the room in a vigorous Russian dance which ended in a double somersault and a Catherine wheel. The somersault was superb but the Catherine wheel was disastrous and he landed full length on three of us, knocking us to the floor. Everyone else shrieked with joy and shouted "More! More!" Competition was now so keen that soon everybody was showing off and there was no audience left to watch them.

When we were all exhausted, we sat down and called on the children to entertain us. This was a much graver affair. The 14-year-old daughter of the house did a dance accompanied by her brother on the drum. It seemed to me a great pity that she was dressed in European clothes, for her short, rather tight, blue skirt did not exactly lend itself to an Oriental dance. When she had finished we all applauded, but I suspected that most people thought their own performance had been much better and they all began offering to do another turn. The general vote was for a double-turn by the bun-faced woman and her husband. They leaped up with alacrity and did a dance in which she was the man and he the woman. It ended two minutes later in floods of hysterics on both sides. Then our hostess announced that dinner was ready.

We went into the room next door where we found two tables loaded down with food. When we sat down, the children brought in more food — hot dishes like kabobs that had to be eaten quickly. In no time my plate was overflowing, as everybody pressed on me what they imagined to be the most English delicacy. Persian dishes with the same name change a lot from one region to the next. Here in Tabriz the little rolls of vine leaves stuffed with, I think, brains were particularly good. I had never liked them before.

After dinner the ladies put on their *chadors* and *pichehs* and we went out to have a drink. By this time it was past midnight, and when we reached the tavern it was shut and showed no signs of opening for us; so we had a dance in the street. The darkness gave me confidence and I attempted to do an Irish jig, but I cannot have been very successful for soon afterwards the party broke up.

When I told Shirin and Faiz next morning that I was going to have lunch with the two brothers from the bus, Faiz insisted on sending a French-speaking clerk from his office with me. This rather spoilt things, for the ladies could not eat with us and I had to go back and forth between the men's and the women's sides of the house and could not do justice to a really excellent lunch. I also felt that I had somehow disappointed them; the interpreter was quite unnecessary, as we had understood each other well enough on the bus. It was just one of those well-meaning blunders that are so difficult to avoid.

Next day I asked Shirin out to lunch. Her husband disapproved, but as he was going to be out all day we thought he need not know. She said good-bye to her daughter and granddaughter as if she were starting on a round-the-world trip. Then, in a state of high excitement, with her *picheh* pulled well over her face and her *chador* tightly gripped between her teeth, she crept out of the back door.

I had chosen a Russian restaurant, for I wanted everything to be as unlike Persia as possible. We arrived without mishap. The first thing which caught her eye when we sat down at the table was one of those little bells which ring when you hit the top, and I had to explain what it was for. The waiter arrived and we had some difficulty in ordering, for I could not read Russian and knew nothing about Russian food, but at last a meal of some sort was ordered. No sooner had the waiter turned his back than she dropped her *chador* for a moment and hit the bell a most terrific crack. Everybody in the room jumped at the noise while she let out a peal of laughter and hid her head under the table. She came up a second or two later, digging me in the ribs and pointing at the bell.

Then the food arrived and created a new difficulty, for when the waiter tried to hand it to her on the right side she turned her head away and drew her *chador* across her face. This effectively prevented her from seeing the dish, so he hurried round to the other side, but again she turned away. This looked like going on for ever, so I took the dish and helped her myself. Then, cautiously holding her *chador* in one hand, she tried to feed herself with the other, but as her meat was too big to be eaten until it was cut up, she kept having to drop her *chador* so that she could use both hands. At once a man would come into view and down would go knife and fork all over again. And unfortunately she did not like any of the foreign food that I thought she would enjoy. So in the end we called for *mast* and oranges, and when she had eaten five of them she said it was time to go home.

That night we went out to another soirée, which was identical with the last. Even the guests were the same — for there cannot be much variety when you can only ask your relations — but everybody enjoyed themselves just as much.

Next morning a Mr. Iftakar arrived and told me he had been sent by Faiz to show me round the town.

"Where would you like to go?" he asked me in English.

"I should like to see the covered bazaars," I replied.

But he seemed to have his own ideas of what we should do. While I walked along at a brisk pace he kept trying to hail droshkies. I complimented him on his English and was a bit surprised when he said, "Well, you see, I'm an American College boy."

This turned out to mean that he had been educated by American missionaries.

"The Head of College is a very nice boy," he went on, "a great pal of mine. We'll go see him later today. But first I guess you'd like a drink, it's so hot out here."

We sat down at the first café and had two very gassy lemonades. Then he went on trying to hail a droshky. I protested again.

"But Faiz gave me two dollars to spend on droshkies," he replied, "and I sure don't want to let him down."

So I relented. We got into the droshky, but before he told the driver where to go, he turned to me.

"Have you got your camera with you?" he asked.

"Yes."

"Then I'll take you some place where you can get a very nice photograph."

We drove to the centre of the town where there was an old ruined wall. I dare say it had some historical importance, but all I can now remember is that it was very old, very ruined and made entirely of mud.

"There's a stairway to the top," said Mr. Iftakar, when he had paid off the droshky, "so we can walk right up and you can take your photo from the top."

When we reached the foot of the stairs we were confronted by a nailed-up wooden door and a large wooden notice forbidding us to enter. Mr. Iftakar was not deterred. He took off one of his shoes and began to hammer on the door with it. This had no effect on the door but the noise soon attracted a policeman, who pointed out that the notice said no one was allowed to go up.

"Yes, yes," replied Mr. Iftakar, "but I have been asked to show the English lady round Tabriz, and I want to take her up the tower."

"Of course, of course," replied the policeman, and turning to me he said, "You may go up, Madame, but you must not take any photographs."

Then he produced a small axe and smashed open the door. We plodded up the stairs, Mr. Iftakar counting, "One, two, three, four," for my benefit all the way up to 250. When we got to the top he hurried me round to the other side.

"Here the parapet will hide you from the policeman," he said, "so you can go right ahead and take your photographs."

I set my camera and pointed it at the view, only to find that Mr. Iftakar had planted himself straight in front of me with an arm pointing out over Tabriz. He filled the whole picture. But there was nothing I could do, so I just took his photo, and as it was the last exposure on my film, we turned round and plodded downstairs again. He hailed another droshky and this time he took me to the bazaars.

The bazaars were long alleys with domed roofs, like those I had already seen in Teheran. I began buying provisions to stock up for my journey across Russia: dried peaches stuffed with almonds and sugar, others stuffed with some kind of dried molasses, and quantities of dates, figs, pistachio nuts and almonds. The whole lot cost no more than two shillings and they lasted me a month. I also wanted to buy some of the lovely socks knitted of wool of many different colours which I had seen the peasants wearing. But Mr. Iftakar insisted that they were low and common things and refused to let me buy them. A little farther on he capitulated and let me buy a pipe for a farthing. He did all the bargaining and it took half an hour in four different shops before this purchase was completed.

"If I had been alone," he told me, "it would have all been over in ten minutes. But you're a foreigner and that makes all the difference."

Having done my shopping I asked him to take me to the police station so that I could get my passport put in order before I finally left Persia.

"By the way," I confided to him, "the police are sure to want a photograph of me, and I've only got one left. I started with 14 but the police have taken one at every police station I've called at. I must keep this one; I'll need it in Russia."

"That's O.K., that's O.K.," he assured me. "The police are very nice boys, great friends of mine." And off he went to the police station. It was not easy to find, for there had been a big flood a few months before and it had dissolved the mud houses in that area and most of them had collapsed. We climbed over the remains of three mud houses and up a little wooden ladder onto a very rickety verandah. This was the police station. In the first room we found one of Mr. Iftakar's very nice boys. He had a face like a lemon and betrayed not the slightest interest when he was told what we wanted; he just went on writing; we might not have been there. After three minutes of silence, the lemon uttered two brief words.

"We're in the wrong room," Mr. Iftakar explained. "It's all O.K., he's a nice boy... a great friend of mine."

This scene was repeated in three more rooms with three more "nice boys" until we came to a large office with several clerks. Here at last we were welcomed, the boys were really nice and really great friends. Of course they could not do anything for us themselves, but they did manage to interest somebody higher up, and then the battle began.

"We must have your photograph," they said, as I knew they would.

"I have none left."

"You cannot leave Persia until you have given us your photograph."

"I have given 13 photographs of myself to the police already — surely that is enough!"

And so it went on. Meanwhile Mr. Iftakar rallied all the really nice boys to our side, and when four of them all began to talk at once, the opposition crumbled and the winning side carried off the stamped passport to the nearest tea-shop to celebrate the victory. I was glad when at last Mr. Iftakar hailed yet another droshky to drive me home.

The passport photograph.

CHAPTER SEVEN
ACROSS THE ARAXES

WHEN Faiz and Shirin saw my passport and realized that I really was going to Russia, they quickly organized a party to dissuade me. Each guest had a fearful tale of what had happened to some friend of a friend, but perhaps the worst fate with which I was threatened was that I would be kidnapped and used as a brood-mare by the "Organization for Improving the Physique of the Russian Nation". They nearly made me change my mind, not because of their horror stories but because of their obvious terror of Russia. There was nothing artificial about it.

So when the day came for me to start, I felt as if I was going to my execution. Shirin had assembled a mass of provisions, being determined that I should at least arrive at the border fit and well. They sent me off to Julfa, the frontier town, in their own car, loaded down with supplies: three chickens wrapped in bread, all my nuts and fruit, a dozen hard-boiled eggs, some oranges, and a bottle of attar of roses.

The first hitch occurred at the police station outside Tabriz. We had to show all our passes and papers before they would let us out, and something seemed wrong with some of them. I feared that it must be mine, for I still had a guilty conscience after my struggle with the police about the photograph, so I interrupted the flood of Persian between the driver and the policeman and found out by pointing in turn to myself, the driver, and the car, that I was "good" but the driver and the car were "not good". So I stayed in the police station, and the driver took the car back to town to get the missing permits. After I had spent three-quarters of an hour of sitting on the roof of the police station and lugubriously gazing at a field, the driver appeared with a policeman and we were allowed to go on.

I had left Tabriz with fear in my heart but sunshine in the sky. As we approached the Russian frontier, the sky became overcast; when we were still six miles from Julfa the most terrific wind sprang up and it started to rain. I was bitterly cold and put on my *poshteen*, a sheepskin coat, but it hardly made any difference.

At Julfa we made for the stationmaster's house, for I had been given a letter of introduction to him. We found him sitting in his garden and keeping himself from being blown out of his seat by holding on to the table in front of him. When I presented my letter he tried to stand up but had to sit down again at once, for he seemed quite unable to cope with the wind. He was the thinnest person I have ever seen, so his fear of being blown away was understandable. Somehow he managed to hang on safely to himself and to the letter while he read it. Then he struggled manfully to his feet and said, "I will come with you to the Customs post, Madame, and take you to the bridge over the Araxes, which is our frontier with Russia."

I was already prepared for the Customs. I had been treated so hospitably in Persia and had had to buy so little for myself that I had a good deal of Persian money left over. I expected I should have some trouble about taking it out of the country so I thought it better to hide the big notes in my bag and to admit only to the small change. It was just as well I did, because the Customs immediately took away the two shillings I admitted to having and gave them to a porter who was waiting to carry my bag. Then they started to look through my luggage but soon lost interest, shut it up and told me I could go.

So we began to cross the bridge — the stationmaster, the porter with my bag, and I. When we were only a third of the way across the Araxes, a gust of wind knocked over the fragile stationmaster, who lay flat on his stomach while the porter dropped my bag and ran to help him. When the stationmaster had been lifted to his feet he obviously felt that he had done all he could. The two men waved good-bye to me and made their way back across the bridge to the Persian side, the porter now carrying the stationmaster.

I felt pretty forlorn as I watched them go, when suddenly I heard a shout behind me and turned to find a Russian soldier advancing. He went on shouting so I supposed he must want my passport. I pulled it out and tried to give it him, but what with the wind and everything blowing about, we lost it and, to my horror, I saw it sailing away across the bridge towards the water. It seemed as if nothing could stop it, and I began to have visions of myself dying on the bridge, unable either to go on into Russia or back into Persia, when it caught in a railing. We both rushed after it, screaming at the tops of our voices, and the soldier retrieved it. He put it in his pocket and walked back. Then he picked up my bag and we crossed to the Russian side.

There I was taken into a guard-house, and for the first time on my journey I realized I had made some progress with my Persian, for I was most surprised to hear myself making a long and apparently fluent speech in that language. But they knew not a word of Persian, and I had absolutely no Russian, so we soon gave up trying to talk to one another and I offered them cigarettes instead.

While we were making friends, a man came in who looked much more like what I was expecting than any of the others did. His hair was cropped short like a German's, and he had high Slav cheekbones. I think he must have been in charge of the Customs post; at all events he at once began to cross-question me, but I had no idea what he was talking about. He told the others to open my bag, and while they were doing so, he led me over to the wall where there were pictures of various sorts of currency — English, French, Persian and American. He pointed to my bag, making it quite clear he wanted to know if I had any, so I pulled out my travellers' cheques and displayed them with great pride, trying to explain that it was all I had got. He then pointed to the English notes on the wall — the American and the Persian. Each time I denied having any with the greatest vigour. Then I sat down and pulled out my knitting. This seemed to have a very soothing effect. For the first time he smiled, then he sat down at his desk and started filling in the details of my passport. While he was doing this I laid my handbag on the table, forgetting that in one of the pockets were all the Persian notes that I had denied having.

The other men seemed to be having trouble with my baggage, so I went over to help them, only to find that what had held them up was merely amazement at the sight of my oranges. While my back was turned, the head man must have opened the handbag I had left on the table and it did not take him long to find all the

Persian notes, which amounted to about eight pounds. His exclamation made me turn round, and he held up the notes in front of my face, obviously asking what they were. As casually as I could I said *"pul"* — which is the Persian for money — and tried to look innocent. All the other soldiers looked up. They had stopped smiling and looked very grave, and I thought I was going to be taken to prison. The head man then gave orders for my bag to be searched properly and everything was taken out and thrown on the floor. This seemed to make them feel better and when I handed round the stuffed peaches and they had each taken one, things began to look a little brighter. I think they must have come to the conclusion that I was a drivelling idiot. One of them took my Persian money and wrote out a long list of it on a piece of paper. Then the head man put the money into my hand, folded my fingers over it and made signs to me to hold it like that until I reached the other Russian frontier — which I did not expect to do for another three weeks.

At this moment there was suddenly a fearful clattering outside, and we all rushed to the window to find an old lorry driving up, the radiator cap gone and steam spurting up a foot in the air. The soldiers at once started throwing all my things back in the bag and putting on their hats and coats. Then they seized me by the arms and hurried me into the lorry. I was put in front, next to the driver, with a soldier on the other side. Two other soldiers with fixed bayonets stood on the steps, and the head man and three others behind.

We rattled our way to the town of Julfa, arriving outside the Intourist office in clouds of steam. Nobody in the Intourist spoke either French or Persian, but they showed me to my room and called me back to say good-bye to the soldiers who were very friendly. I shook hands with them all, and they got back in the lorry and drove off.

The Intourist people, a man and a woman who were running a small bar with a few bedrooms off it for stray visitors, were very puzzled by me. When they gave me the visitors' book to sign, I saw that I was the third foreigner to have come through Julfa, the others being an Italian and a Turk.

Behind the bar, and four steps up, was a raised passage, with five bedrooms opening off it like loose-boxes beyond stable doors cut in halves at the middle so the top would open separately. The

Intourist couple were very kind to me; they took me into the bar and gave me a glass of tea from a samovar, and we were trying to start a conversation when a man in uniform arrived and looked at me with great disgust. He asked for my passport and did not seem to like that either. Then he spoke sharply to the Intourist people and went out. They looked very upset; the woman took my hand, led me back to the bedroom, where she pushed me gently in and went away, locking the door behind her.

This was rather upsetting, and I sat down on the bed and tried to make a plan but could not think of one, for I did not know what was wrong. I had not had time to find out which days the train ran to Tiflis or what time it left; all I had learnt from the Intourist office in Teheran was that it did not run daily. I had plenty of food but there was no water in the room. I should have to slake my thirst on oranges, of which I still had eight. What annoyed me most was that I had nothing to read, for I had finished all the books I had brought from India and had not been able to get any English books from the Persians I had stayed with. There was still my knitting, but that had its limitations.

I decided to wait for an hour before trying to get out of my room. I unpacked my food and started to arrange it on a table to see what I could spare for bribes. By the time I had finished I had given myself such an appetite that I ate a whole cooked chicken.

Just as I was licking my fingers over the last bones, the top half of the door opened and the Intourist woman looked in. She had a friendly smile and carried a glass of tea and a piece of black bread. I went over and took the tea gratefully while I held up an orange in the other hand. She looked longingly at the orange, so I pushed the top half of the door wide open and then peeled the orange and offered her half, trying to make her understand that in exchange she must leave the top half of the door open. She gave a little nod of her head and shut the door. I heard her running down the steps to the bar, and in no time she was back with the man. She pointed to the orange and the door, and after a moment's indecision he nodded his head and reached for the orange. As there were two of them I gave them it all.

I felt I had made great progress, so I put away my food in case the people in the bar might see it and start asking for something. As I sat knitting in the lighted bedroom with the lower half of the door locked, people from the bar came up and tried to talk to me, so I got out a pencil and paper and tried to draw a clock and a train, saying "Tiflis" over and over again in hopes someone would understand me. At last they did, and I was horrified to learn that the train started at five the next morning.

By the time we had finished drawing clocks and trains I was on very friendly terms with a couple of young men, and they asked me to dance. I pointed to the locked door. One of them went away and came back with the Intourist man. He was holding a bit of orange in his hand and made signs that if I gave him another I could come out. So I gave him another and he unlocked the door. The two young men escorted me to a table in the bar where they danced with me in turn till I nearly died of exhaustion, for the dances were very lively and quick and there was lots of swinging round and round.

After an hour of this there was nobody else left in the bar, and when the Intourist man and woman came and sat at our table I said that I had danced enough for one night and brought out my pencil and paper to find out whether I should be allowed to catch my train in the morning or have to stay locked in my room. After a good deal of inexpert scribbling I understood them to mean that they would let me go, and indeed that they would wake me up at half-past four in the morning and take me to the station. By now it was past midnight, so I said a hurried good night and went to bed.

Next morning they woke me up at a quarter to five with a glass of tea. It was just like Persia: you had to be awash with tea before you were allowed to do anything. At a quarter past five we started for the station, which turned out to be only five minutes away. There was not a sign of life there, and though the train was drawn up in the station we were not allowed to get into it. I guessed I was in for a long wait, so I brought out my knitting. Soon there were half a dozen women gathered round me watching. I recognized one of them as a fellow guest from the Intourist Hotel and found that she too was going on the train. When at last we were allowed into the train we got into the same carriage. She was travelling with two children and a nurse, and her husband had come to see her off.

When the train had started, we began trying to talk to one another in earnest. She knew one or two words of Persian and I tried to get her to teach me some Russian. The first and most important phrase I learnt was the Russian words for "no money".

Then came *kharasho,* which seemed to mean "O.K." or "fine, fine," and was used of almost anything that was going well.

Then we unpacked our baggage and began showing one another our clothes. She was very interested in anything woollen and was fascinated by my silk stockings, powder and lipstick, which she said were very bad in Russia. In her luggage I found a little medical syringe in a tin. This, she explained, was for morphia and proceeded to give herself an injection, saying something about her husband being a doctor. She injected herself three times with the stuff while I was with her. Whenever we stopped at a station she would take me with her to fetch boiling water for making tea. Each station had a special tap for it.

The train was fairly empty till we got to Erivan, the capital of Armenia, but then our carriage filled to bursting. The doctor's wife, who had told me before we reached Erivan that she did not like Armenians, moved to another carriage. I could see no reason for her dislike; at all events the Armenians who got into the carriage seemed very nice people to me. There were two married couples. One of the men wore a double-breasted blue serge suit, and at first glance looked like an Englishman with his blue eyes and fair hair, his broad shoulders and tidy, freshly shaved face. His wife had obviously been a pretty girl but had grown rather plump. The other couple consisted of a large, fat, mannish-looking woman with a tiny, thin husband who was nattily dressed in a spotless, blue silk Russian blouse with a white cord round his waist and a blue silk yachting cap on his head. They looked very prosperous. There was also a large, friendly young man in a Russian blouse; he was much less tidy and prosperous-looking than the others.

Directly the train started, they tried to find out who and what I was. Having been primed by the Persians, I disclaimed any connection with the British Army or capitalists. After two hours' hard work, I managed to put it across to them that I was the wife of a proletariat engineer working for a capitalist textile firm in Bombay. I was going from India to England to visit my two brothers, one of whom was a farmer and the other a clerk. I thoroughly recommend anyone travelling through Russia to claim some relationship to an engineer — though perhaps engineers are not quite so popular now as they were then. The Russian word for engineer must be much the same as the English; at all events they all understood me: as soon as I said "engineer" the whole carriage stood up as one man and shouted *"Kharasho! Kharasho!"* The young man in the double-breasted blue suit was also an engineer, so we had to shake hands on that. Then we started exchanging names and words. They wanted to know how people addressed each other in England, and when I told them, they found "Mr." and "Mrs." hysterically funny — perhaps with good reason. The tiny husband was particularly delighted; he kept nudging me and pointing at his huge wife until I said "Mrs.". Then he would clap his hands and laugh so helplessly that he was hardly able to say *"Kharasho! Kharasho!"* When he had recovered he would start pointing at himself and nudging me till I said "Mr.", and the whole thing would begin all over again.

The friendly and untidy young man began bringing out his lunch. By now I was well trained in Persian hospitality, so I brought mine out and started to offer it round. They were very indignant at this and made me put all my food away again, insisting that I should eat only theirs. I was given the whole of a small pink fish rather like a trout. They said it had been caught in Lake Gokcha and was a speciality of Erivan.

Two more men joined us while we were eating our meal. One of them looked like a small red rat in a natty suit, the other was a soulful young man with enormous brown eyes. When we had finished eating, the red rat started to talk to me. I could not understand what he was saying; it seemed to be something to do with the first class — for Russian trains were not a classless society.

"No money!" I replied at once, with my words pat.

Thereupon the red rat gave up trying to talk directly to me and started putting his proposition to the rest of the people in the carriage. A tremendous argument began, with the mild little married man taking my part and the hearty young man supporting the red rat. At least that is what I thought was happening. After a good deal of pantomime and screaming of *"Kharasho!"* I at last understood that the red rat was offering to sleep in the third class while I took his place in the first class. All my travelling companions kept repeating "International Wagons-Lits, *Kharasho! Kharasho!"* urging me by signs to go and see for myself. I sat tight and patted the wooden seat, saying, *"Kharasho! Kharasho!"* But this did not satisfy them; they seemed to want me at least to go and have a look.

So I let the red rat escort me away up the train. We walked on and on through the second class and the dining-car till we finally reached the Holy of Holies, the Wagons-Lits. A guard stood at the entrance to the coach, and he had to unlock the door before we could go through. There did not seem to be a single person in the whole coach, and the coupé we went into was quite unoccupied. The red rat hit the seat hard and said *"Kharasho!"* to show me how good the springing was. Then he pointed to himself, saying, "Doctor, medicine," and I replied *"Kharasho!"* We sat down and he pointed out of the window at a great, snow-covered mountain, which I had seen for some time, and said "Ararat". I was trying to think of something else to keep the conversation going when he suddenly seized me round the throat and made a noise like "Ah! Ah!" I did not quite know what was happening, but I thought I had better go on behaving as if it were all perfectly normal. I tried to say "Ah! Ah!" too, like a dutiful patient, but he was choking me so much that it was not easy. Fortunately he released my throat and seized my wrist, feeling for my pulse and muttering "Doctor, doctor," all the time. Then he started on my reflexes, crossing my legs and hitting them below the knee-cap; the right leg was *"Kharasho"*, the left *"Niet kharasho"*. After all this he flung himself on his knees at my feet and, I thought, asked me to stay with his mummy at Tiflis. As the only words I understood were "Mummy" and "Tiflis" I may have been mistaken. However, I firmly said *"Niet!"* Then he sat down beside me and tried to put his arm round me, but I promptly stood up so that he had to let go, for he was a very small man. His next proposition, if I understood him aright, was that we should both spend the night in the first class. I replied *"Niet!"* loudly and firmly and made for the door.

I went out into the passage and started the walk back to the third class. He came close behind me, plucking at my blouse and talking without a pause. I stalked on as majestically as I could in the swaying and bumping train, every now and then throwing a *"Niet!"* over my shoulder. He talked on and on, but I understood not a word until we came to the restaurant car, when I suddenly heard him say "Vodka".

"Niet!" I replied automatically, before I could stop myself.

"Champagne!" he shouted in a last desperate bid to stop me.

"Niet!" I said again — and immediately regretted it.

But I could not change my mind now, and it was *"Niet! Niet! Niet!"* all the way back to my original compartment. There I was welcomed with cries of joy. I sat down, patted the seat and said *"Wagons-Lits niet kharasho!"*

At this they all turned on the poor red rat and chased him off. We settled down again and the soulful young man whipped out a balalaika and started to play some lovely haunting songs. One of the couples brought out some tea, and the rest of us started singing too. After some Armenian, Georgian and Russian songs, the young man announced in tones of pride: "Fox-trot — English — *Mr. Brown.*" Fortunately I recognized "How do you do - do - do - Mr. Brown?" and I could tell them a few of the words in English. They were delighted. After "Mr. Brown" we tried "The Blue Danube", and though it was now past ten at night, the party showed no signs of breaking up.

They asked to see my ring and watch, and this started another pantomime as they explained what fearful thieves the people of Tiflis were. The man in the suit acted me, while the rest pretended to steal my jewellery and run off with it. Then they found *One's Company* by Peter Fleming, which I had been re-reading. Unfortunately they opened it, quite by chance, at a picture of an anti-communist poster. I hastily turned over the pages and tried to distract their attention by showing them another picture, but the next one I came to was a photograph of the wreck of the Trans-Siberian Express. There was nothing for it but to sit down firmly on the book, murmuring as always, *"Kharasho, kharasho"*. I yawned in an exaggeratedly pointed manner and tried to go to sleep, and I was delighted when they took the hint and settled themselves down for the night.

While I was struggling with a Russian lesson next morning with four or five instructors each with his own method of teaching, the train slowed up and stopped. We all crowded to the window to see where we were. The train had halted just outside a station. There seemed to be some trouble up by an engine in a siding. A little knot of people were gathered there. While I was looking at them they moved apart, and I saw two men with a stretcher come out and start to walk along the track beside our train. They passed just below our window and there, in the dirtiest stretcher I have ever seen, a man lay dying. He seemed to be unconscious, and his face, which was only faintly smeared with blood, was calm and still. His right arm and leg rested whole and sound on the edge of the stretcher, but his left side was tragic, just an awful jumble of clothes, bones, flesh and blood. As he passed underneath us he slowly turned his head, opened his eyes and gazed unseeingly up at us. I felt suddenly ashamed of staring at him like that and climbed hurriedly back into my seat.

At once all the Russians began to talk at the tops of their voices. They turned to me, waving their arms and gesticulating, to ask what I thought of it all.

"Niet kharasho," I replied feebly, being totally unable to express what I really felt.

They all burst out laughing and clapped their hands as if the whole thing had been arranged to test my Russian. They had been so kind to me that this merry callousness seemed quite incredible.

The man in the blue suit, who had gone out to see if he could find out what had happened, now came back and told us all about it, but the only words I could understand were "machine" and "engineer", which was not much help.

When the train arrived at Tiflis, we all got out together, and the people in my compartment all stayed with me and talked till the Intourist agent found me. At the time I thought nothing of it, but it was the only time it happened to me in Russia. The Intourist man commandeered a porter for my baggage and we walked to the hotel, which turned out to be quite different from the one at Julfa, for it had a grand portico and handsome marble steps, all very dirty, and had obviously been built in Tsarist times. There was a wash-basin in my bedroom with taps for h. and c., but the h. did not run at all and the c. was very sporadic. I was terribly bored by Tiflis. This was no fault of the place itself but because nobody but the Intourist man ever spoke to me, and he only did so because he was paid to. Outside my bedroom he never left me alone for a second. We walked for miles while he showed me the town and the official sights, and it was as dreary a chore for me as it was for him. I was heartily glad the next evening when I could join the train for the journey to Batum.

As long as the Intourist man remained in the train with me, everybody was silent. But as soon as the train started to move he had to jump out, and then everybody in the compartment gathered round me and began to ask questions. When they grasped that I was English they searched the whole train for somebody who could speak my language. They brought along several people who spoke German, but I, unfortunately, did not. At last after a long search they found a man who could speak French. He sat down with us and interpreted my answers to all the usual questions. I trotted out my engineer husband in Bombay and the brothers in England, and it all went down very well. Then he asked me to go to his carriage, so we walked off but stood in the corridor instead, and he began telling me about the new Russia. He was the first person I had met on a train who had been outside Russia. All the others thought everything was wonderful and that all other countries were very backward by comparison. He was also older than most of the people I had talked to, and he had seen a great deal. Moreover, he had spent five years in Paris. I asked him what the new Russia was really like.

"It is much better now," he replied. "When the five-year plan started, the suffering was terrible. All imports were strictly prohibited. There was no wool, and in the winter it was bitterly cold. When someone was dying, the relatives would sit round waiting for him to die so that they could divide his clothes. Sometimes they did not even wait for him to die. But all that is finished now and I think that each year things will get a little better."

We were still in the corridor talking when the train stopped at a station. An enormous peasant woman got in, a baby at her breast, her bovine face without the least glimmer of intelligence.

He looked at her and said, "In the old days these women used to come on the train and drop their unwanted babies out of the window, but the Revolution has made that unnecessary with free abortion. The Russian peasant is quite different from the European women; she spends all her extra money on food — it is her only interest; they spend it on clothes."

I asked him if he would like to go back to France.

"Of course," he replied, "but they will not let me leave Russia now — and I do not think they will ever give me permission to do so."

I felt very sorry for him, virtually imprisoned in a country about which he had no illusions.

"I would not have talked to you like this," he went on, "but I know that there is nobody on the train who understands French. Please do not recognize me if we meet outside the train at Batum; it may be dangerous for me."

We said good-bye, and I never saw him again.

CHAPTER EIGHT
"COMRADE, A WALL!"

We arrived at Batum in the morning, and sure enough there was an Intourist man on the station waiting for me. He took me straight to the hotel, an attractive, one-storeyed building with a patio. Batum itself was a sleepy Black Sea port, and the Intourist people also seemed far more languorous and free-and-easy than they had been in Tiflis. They let me walk about by myself and offered me free drinks every now and then. I had a ticket which was supposed to cover the cost of my sightseeing, so I showed it to them and asked what I could see.

"This entitles you to see the hospital in the old Tsarist Palace," they told me, "and for another 30 roubles we will take you to see the Botanical Gardens."

That made me dig my toes in. "No money," I said, "except Persian money."

They had never accepted Persian money and they did not do so now. The man went out of the room and I could hear him discussing me in the next room. When he came back he was smiling.

"You can go anyway, you need not pay," he said. "Please be at this office punctually at two-thirty."

At two-thirty punctually I walked across the patio to the office. I heard an American woman's voice loud and clear: "Last time I was in Europe, Thomas Cook fixed my trip, and when I tell you that from May to October I never had more than five minutes to myself you will realize my time is valuable."

I did not catch the reply to this, but the interpreter came out so eagerly to greet me that I felt sure that this Mrs. Davis — as I found she was called — was responsible for my free Botanical Gardens trip.

An open car was waiting outside and it took the three of us — Mrs. Davis, the guide and me — to the Botanical Gardens. They looked to me pretty much the same as any other botanical gardens but perhaps a bit more untidy. Then we went to the hospital. It was outside the town, standing in its own lovely grounds with big trees and grass sweeping right round them. The building was fine, too, with marble columns and a huge hall and reception rooms, now filled with hospital beds. The guide was obviously very proud of it, though to me it looked rather grubby and disorganized. There were hardly any nurses and no furniture at all except the beds. The patients all looked very cheerful. For them it was wonderful medicine just to be in bed in one of the Tsar's summer palaces and not to have to pay a penny for it.

Mrs. Davis was horrified by everything she saw, but as she addressed all her remarks to me, the guide remained filled with pride. Her heart was not really in the sightseeing; she was too worried about the rest of her itinerary. She had always travelled in a group, she said, but in Russia her group had somehow or other gradually disintegrated until she was on her own. Now she expected the Intourist to produce another group for her to travel with. I could see that both she and the Intourist were in for a hard time of it, and I was very glad I was travelling third for otherwise they might have co-opted me to make up a group for her.

That evening my boat left for Yalta and I was shot of them both. My accommodation was not too bad — a berth in a large cabin with about ten other women. I do not remember much of the first part of the journey; it passed in a daze. I had a high temperature, brought on by food poisoning and perhaps a touch of malaria. Soon I was too weak to walk to the lavatory and had to resort to crawling on hands and knees while the other passengers took no notice of my lowly progress along the floor except to get out of my way. However, one of them must have told a doctor because while lying in bed I felt a thermometer being put in my mouth. I opened my eyes to find a man in a uniform cap standing beside me.

"Doctor, doctor," he said and pointed to himself.

"India, malaria," I replied, and after that I do not remember any more.

Next day I felt much better — well enough to sit up in bed and try to do my hair. Immediately my cabin mates flocked round me, offering grapes, looking-glasses, towels and soap. They were all very kind and one of them even brought me some dreary soup and black bread. In the end they let me sleep for a couple of hours but then woke me up and urged me to get dressed and go on deck.

A space had been cleared on deck so that people could dance to the music of an accordion. As soon as I arrived, tottering and clinging to the arm of a stalwart Russian girl, four or five men rushed up and asked me to dance. I wanted nothing more than a chance to sit down, but they would not have any of that. They took it in turn to carry me round the floor, my legs hardly touching the deck and only very occasionally supporting me. When they realized I really was far too exhausted to dance, they took me to a table where they gave me wine and tried to make conversation.

Progress was very slow, as my brain was quite addled with exhaustion and illness. Several people came up and began speaking German, only to depart frustrated. Then at last the most magnificent sight appeared — a tall figure in a long, pale blue, tight-waisted overcoat, military cap, boots and spurs. He came and took my hand and said in clear English, "Good morning, Comrade."

I replied with a torrent of English, falsely assuming that he knew the language perfectly — a mistake which has infuriated me when *I* have been haltingly trying to speak a foreign language.

He listened to me with his face a perfect blank. Then for five minutes he frowned in fearful concentration before he at last brought out the words: "Stop, correct."

I waited, puzzled, for more to come.

Again there was a fearful pause while we all gazed at him.

"I speak not much English uncorrect," he said. "I do not speak English correct."

I was now beginning to get the hang of the conversation and replied encouragingly, "Correct, correct."

The conversation went ahead like this, very very slowly, and after we had been at it for an hour and a half, he had understood what I was doing and I had learnt that he was a colonel in the Red Army, aged 26, and that Madame Litvinoff had been teaching him English.

What with the fever and the dancing, an hour and a half of this struggling conversation was enough and I persuaded the girl who had brought me up on deck to take me back to bed.

Next day when the boat docked at Yalta, there was the inevitable Intourist man waiting on the quay. He took me to the hotel, where I had a real hot bath for the first time in Russia. The meal afterwards was none too good, but my appetite was still so poor that it hardly mattered. Then I went out and walked along the beach, where I met the officer again. He asked me to dine with him. I was thrilled and promptly accepted. He ground out the information that he would call for me at six-thirty, and we parted.

Punctually at six-thirty he arrived, and I was much disappointed to see that he had changed his uniform for a checked shirt, blue cotton trousers and a pair of sand-shoes. We left the hotel and started walking along the front. I saw that he was trying to speak so did not say anything myself. It was a fearful strain watching him. Beads of sweat started out on his forehead and I could almost hear him thinking. Suddenly he stopped and clutched my arm. He pointed to a house with his other hand and said, "Comrade, a wall!"

"Comrade, a roof!" I replied, pointing to the roof.

A little farther on we sat down on a bench in some gardens and watched the crowd. Three small boys of about 12 came by, wearing military uniform.

"Comrade, Red Army men!" he said, pointing at them. After this our conversation became quite brisk, and we even began discussing the relative merits of blondes and brunettes.

Then he took me to a small restaurant with tables on the pavement, and we sat outside to eat. I could not read the menu, so I said, "Comrade, a borsch!" Fortunately it did not seem to be etiquette to talk while one was eating, so we could both relax during dinner. Afterwards we walked slowly back to the hotel.

Next morning the Intourist told me that there was something wrong with my ticket and that I must leave at once for Sebastopol. My ticket was good for the local bus but they were so keen to get rid of me that they sent me over alone in one of the Intourist cars without even asking me to pay extra. At the Sebastopol Intourist office I found five Russian tourists with whom I was taken to see the panorama of the Siege of Sebastopol.

"Now we are going to see the ruins," the guide told me, "and for this you must pay five roubles."

The rest of the party had apparently already paid their whack.

"I only have Persian money," I said, producing some of it.

There was the usual confabulation, and then: "It does not matter if you cannot pay, you can go all the same."

We were driven along a broad, dusty road out of the town. I sat in the front with one tourist and the driver, while the other four crowded in behind. There was a shriek from the back as one of the women's hats blew off, and we all shouted at the driver.

"Kharasho!" he cried gleefully and spun the wheel round, the tyres screaming as we turned. Hardly slackening speed, he opened the car door, bent down and gallantly picked the hat up from where it lay on the road. He made another dramatic turn, and we were humming along again in the same direction as before.

The ruins were very lovely, but I failed to discover anything about their history except that they were Greek.

In the afternoon I went to the beach, which was packed with workers from all parts of the Soviet Union who had earned free days by exceeding the average output. The men were all dressed in cotton striped pyjamas. The women were more variously dressed except in the sea, and there they bathed naked, which I thought a mistake for none of them had good figures; indeed most of them seemed slightly misshapen, perhaps from overwork and underfeeding, and muscles bulged out from the most unlikely places, giving an extraordinary impression of endurance and brute strength but certainly not beauty. Even the smallest of bathing-dresses would have been a help.

I thought I would try and see if anyone would accept my meal tickets outside an Intourist hotel. I looked at six restaurants before I found one that was not full to bursting. I sat down at a table and showed the waiter my ticket. He pointed to a corner of the menu and I nodded. He soon came back with some watery cabbage soup and followed this with the leg of a goose that smelt very strong. I ate the potatoes round it. While I was eating, I found myself hypnotized by one of the waiters. I kept looking at him but could not think why. He had white hair and a thin, aristocratic, anxious-looking face. Eventually he noticed me staring and became very uneasy, his hands holding a heavy tray began to shake. It was his long, slender fingers that made me realize what had riveted my attention in the first place. All the time I had been in Russia I had seen nothing but peasant and Oriental types. Now I was looking at a survivor of the old régime and the contrast was amazing. He was almost beautiful.

Next morning I left for Kharkov, 24 hours away. The carriage was full, and as usual no one paid any attention to me until the train had left the station. As soon as the platform was behind us, the questions began. By now I was almost fluent with my story of the engineer husband and the farmer and clerk brothers. When they had finished discussing my imaginary relatives, they started on my age.

There were six men and four women in the compartment and they seemed to be between my own age of 28 and 40 years old. When they asked me my age I counted it out on my fingers.

"*Niet! Niet!*" they all cried at once.

The woman next to me, who had a pleasant lined face with dark, deep-set eyes, touched my arm, then pointed to me and started cradling an imaginary baby in her arms. The others laughed and pointed from me back to the baby.

"When? When?" they asked.

I could not make them believe my age. At last I got out my passport, and when they saw the date of my birth written down, they had to believe it. Then they showed me their identity cards, and I shared their surprise. I was the oldest in the carriage. They must have all suffered terribly to have aged so quickly, but they did not seem to be mentally scarred.

I was still feeling the effects of my fever, and by the time the age question was finally settled, I was quite exhausted. So I firmly closed my eyes and went to sleep. I slept like a log until my neighbour woke me up in the morning to say we were arriving at Kharkov.

I had never wanted to go to Kharkov, as it was an entirely Soviet town dedicated to industry. But they would not have let me have a visa if I was merely going to visit historic places. I had to go to one industrial city and Kharkov was the most convenient. It fully realized my worst imaginings. Dreary, dirty, concrete buildings all in squares, divided by broad, unpaved roads, with old papers blowing down them in the cheerless drizzling rain. Fortunately the Intourist woman was charming; she was a large, red-faced, jolly Dutchwoman who, being an ardent Communist, had emigrated to Russia and was apparently perfectly satisfied with everything there except the shoes. She could not get walking shoes to fit her, but somehow she managed to have them sent from Holland once a year, and, astonishingly enough, they always reached her.

She took me to the hotel, which looked as dreary as the rest of Kharkov, but it was much more efficient than any I had been to so far. I had a lovely hot bath before coming down to breakfast and ordering what I thought were fried eggs. To my joy it turned out to be a large dish of caviar. While I was struggling to find the right kind of ticket to pay for it, I noticed a man staring at me. Eventually he came over to me and introduced himself. He was an Italian and offered me the loan of his Russian-English dictionary. The poor man was frantic with loneliness. He was working for an engineering firm, six months in Leningrad, and now six months in Kharkov. Leningrad had not been too bad because there were other Italians there, but in Kharkov he would come back at half-past six each evening to the hotel, after a day at the works, and have dinner quite alone, and then he would sit by himself until it was time to go to bed. No Russians would speak to him out of the office or ask him to their houses, and they refused his invitations to come and have dinner with him at the hotel. Seldom have I seen such a miserable man. He complained that the food upset his stomach, the women's breasts were the wrong shape, the wine undrinkable, and worst of all there were no post-cards in all Kharkov.

"I have searched the town from end to end," he said, "and I have only been able to find two."

I was very touched when he made me a present of his best one.

He asked me to have dinner with him that evening. It was a very pleasant meal and we talked easily together, so I was quite charmed when he leant forward earnestly during a discussion on engineering in Russia to say, "Verily, verily, you are exactly like a Madonna."

The next day the Intourist people said that I must pay them a further nine pounds. There had been a mistake in the ticket: all the food I had eaten, the taxis taking me to and from the stations, the telegrams that had been sent ahead to say I was coming — all these had cost more than they had originally reckoned. I was still in Russia and there would be more expenses to come, therefore they needed nine pounds more and four photographs.

"All this may be true," I replied, "but I have only been to the places I bought tickets for, and I bought the meal tickets which you told me I would need to cover my time in Russia. It is you who insist on taxis, I have never asked for them, but I am willing, in order not to make trouble, to pay what you ask — in Persian money."

The usual head-shaking began at once, and a nice young man, who spoke good English, said, "I see you are tired. Perhaps after a rest you will feel better about it."

I then launched into a long speech accusing the Intourist of robbing innocent tourists, giving them poisoned food, luring them into Russia with bogus cheap tickets, and then refusing to let them leave until their money was gone. The poor man was quite flattened by this tirade and meekly said he would see if he could arrange something.

The Dutchwoman took me off to see the sights of Kharkov. Each factory was drearier than the last. We came back to the hotel to find the English-speaking young man. He told me gravely that the directors of Intourist had agreed to bear the fearful expense I put on them, on condition that I did not go to Kiev, and had four photographs taken. This was a bitter blow, as Kiev was the place I wanted to see most. But I felt I must not give way now, for once I had started to pay, there was no knowing when they would let me stop. I had one last fling at them.

"No Kiev, no photographs — at least not at my expense."

He shook his head. "They are angry," he said. "They may put you in prison."

"If they do they will have to pay for me all the time."

"I think you do not really understand," he said sadly.

Another meeting was summoned, and they finally decided to go to the expense themselves of having me photographed and then to send me straight out of the country.

Next morning I was taken by two Intourist guides, unfriendly ones, in a tram — a proof of my undesirability — to a photomaton room at the poorest end of the town. There were already 20 people standing in the room waiting to be taken, and we joined in at the end of the queue.

I stood behind two flappers who had been waiting for an hour but still had not got their appearance to their liking when their turn came. They were the only Russian women I saw who betrayed any interest in their looks, and they used lipstick and powder quite freely. They climbed on the only chair in the place and had their photograph taken together. The little photographer took as keen an interest in them as they did in themselves and even traced a smile on their lips with his finger.

My turn came next, and I disappointed the photographer by sitting down glowering at him like a bulldog and making signs to him to get on with his job. He lost no time, took various photos and let me go. The Intourists were quite surprised; I think they had been expecting me to make a fuss. They now became very friendly, and when the photographs were ready they gave me three for myself. One of them was upside down, but I do not know why.

We took the tram back to the hotel where we found an enormous crowd waiting to see the Czech Prime Minister, M. Benes, make his state visit. I had heard that he was in Russia but did not realize that he would be in Kharkov and staying at the same hotel as I was. We could not get in until he had come out, so we joined the crowd who had been ordered to come and welcome him. We waited for ten minutes until two people appeared at the door of the hotel, looked out and hurriedly disappeared. Then, after another wait, a tall, bearded figure in lounge suit and cap came out and stood on the steps. The Intourist told me that he was the Russian minister who was travelling with M. Benes. The crowd stood deathly silent — staring. The minister said something in a loud voice, then turned and beckoned to M. Benes, who came out, evidently expecting a reception, with a smile on his face and his hand ready to take his hat off. The bovine crowd went on staring without moving or making a sound. There was an awkward pause and, still in the same deadly silence, Madame Benes, a stout artificial blonde, came out with a startlingly lovely niece. They all stood in a line while the crowd stared until the Russian minister hurried them into waiting cars. As they drove off, the crowd's heads turned as one to watch them go, but there was no expression on any face. Then the crowd dispersed.

That night I left Kharkov. The Dutchwoman took me to the station, but when we got there we were told the train would be an hour late. She was very distressed.

"I am so sorry," she said. "It is very unusual. In Russia the trains are always on time."

My own experience and the unsurprised and patient faces of the other passengers belied her remarks as we sat down on the platform to wait. After 20 minutes all the lights suddenly went out and alarm signals began ringing. The Dutchwoman seized me by the arm and we rushed with all the other passengers into the big entrance hall, where we were joined by a huge mob coming in from the streets and trams. We forced our way into a big restaurant where people were already lying under all the tables and chairs. It was pitch dark, and I stumbled over various bodies before I reached the window and knelt down, since that seemed the proper thing to do.

I looked out of the window: the whole town was in darkness, not a single light showed anywhere. Cars filled with soldiers kept passing, and then there came the noise of aeroplanes. They were quite easy to see, for they flew very low with all their navigation lights on. As they passed over the station, the searchlights picked them up, held them while they turned, and then picked up the next as it came in. There must have been about 30 aeroplanes. The room and the entrance hall were so tightly packed that I could not lower my arms from the window, but the people were all excited and happy. Those who were near enough for me to see were smiling, and I could hear laughter everywhere. They were the only happy crowd I saw in Russia.

Twenty minutes after the last aeroplane had left, the lights went on again. I had completely lost the Dutchwoman, but when I managed to get out and make my way back to where we had been sitting, I found she was already there. She was most indignant because in the excitement I had left my coat behind.

"It might have been stolen," she said.

"What was all that for?" I asked.

"Air-raid practice for the war against Germany."

I thought for a moment that while I had been travelling some fearful international crisis had arisen.

"Good heavens! When?" I asked.

"We do not know," she replied. "We only know that it will come."

All this excitement had made the wait for the train go like a flash. It arrived very soon and was very full so that we had a struggle to find me a seat. Once again I noticed — as I had done at every previous station — that when the train pulled out, more than half of the people waiting for it had been left behind.

Among the people in the carriage was a young Russian soldier who spoke quite a lot of English. He had never been outside Russia but his accent was excellent. We talked a good deal and he explained that it was an army order that every soldier should learn to speak either English, French or German. They could choose which language and he had chosen English.

When we crossed the Dnieper, the passengers started to close all the windows, but one was broken and when they found they could not budge it they all flung themselves on the floor, pulling me down with them. There we lay till the train was clear of the bridge on the other side. I asked the soldier what all the fuss was about.

"It is forbidden to cross the bridge with the windows open," he replied, "and just to make sure, there are sentries stationed on the bridge with orders to shoot at any window that is still open."

The train pulled into Kiev station and waited while M. Benes's special coach was hooked on. There was no crowd this time but a rather peculiar-looking collection of soldiers, which I took to be a guard of honour. They were all dressed alike and stood in a row, but otherwise they had nothing in common. They were holding assorted weapons impartially in either hand, and they juggled with them awkwardly as the train pulled out.

I hung out of the window to see as much of Kiev as I could. I cursed myself for not paying the extra money so that I could visit the town. As the train left the town behind, I caught a glimpse of a few lovely domes, and then across some fields I spotted a wedding procession. The bride wore a high crown and a gay peasant dress.

To console myself I went to the restaurant-car and finished up my meal tickets. There I met an Algerian, and although I was feeling the cold even in my warmest clothes, he wore nothing but a blue beret, a pale green short-sleeved Aertex shirt, thin grey trousers with broad white stripes, and white kid sandals on his bare feet. He was very excited because he had been on a trip to Moscow, Leningrad and Kiev, and had managed to take photographs of the Kremlin and the Dnieper Bridge, which he intended to smuggle through the Customs.

By the time we arrived at the Russian frontier, the Russians had all left the train and there was no one except the Algerian, a German travelling first class, the Benes party and me. From the stories I had heard I was prepared for the most fearful indignities at the Customs, and I was a little disappointed that no one paid the least attention to me. There was a guard of honour forming up for M. Benes, and the officials had their hands full with seeing that his train went off safely.

The German, the Algerian and I were hurried into a special train and put in a first-class compartment with all the windows tight shut. The central heating was full on and it was stiflingly hot. I tried to open one of the windows, but a soldier armed with a rifle and two pistols made such menacing gestures that I thought better of it.

After two hours we arrived at the railway-junction in Poland where the German and the Algerian got into a train that was leaving for Warsaw, while I waited and tried to find out about my train to Lemberg, but without success. I had already been travelling for 24 hours with very little sleep, and I had no Polish, Russian or English money, though I still had the unwanted Persian money. My bag felt too heavy to carry at that time of night and I had been unable to stop a porter from taking it, though I saw no prospect of being able to tip him. When I showed him my Persian money and tried to explain I had nothing else, he took me to a man on the platform who, he said, would change money. But the man had never had anything to do with Persian money and did not want to start now. Various people gathered round to see what was going on and to offer advice. Unfortunately I did not know the value of Polish money and the money-changer did not know the value of the Persian. All the crowd were very lavish with their advice, but it was quite incomprehensible to me until suddenly to my relief I heard someone speaking French, and I turned and saw a little, white-haired old lady. She was like a fairy godmother. She fixed an exchange that satisfied everybody.

"You look tired, my dear," she said and took me to a restaurant.

"Please keep my money," I said, "and buy what you can with it. Just leave me enough to pay for something to eat in Lemberg and tips for porters."

She bought me a huge cup of coffee and two large ham rolls. After Russian food they tasted like ambrosia. As I munched my rolls she went on talking.

"Whenever a train arrives from Russia," she said, "I come to meet it to see if there are any Russian refugees on board. My husband and I, we escaped eight years ago. He is a doctor and now he is doing quite well here in Poland. Not many refugees have escaped lately, but I still always meet the trains. When I saw the crowds round you I thought you must be a refugee."

When I had finished eating, she told me the time my train left and then kissed me good-night and went home. The porter took me across to the platform which was packed with people waiting for the Lemberg train. When it arrived it was even more crammed and there seemed no hope of getting a seat. Fortunately my Russian training stood me in good stead, and with some shrewd kicks and blows I forced my way in and sat down.

Then the real discomfort began, for it was much harder than the lowest class that foreigners were permitted to use in Russia. The carriages were not divided into compartments but were open like a London tube. My particular carriage was filled with a girls' school and three families, each with four children. This was already quite the most uncomfortable part of my journey, but there was worse to come. At four-thirty in the morning, a covey of old women on their way to market stormed the carriage and took it by force. They barged their way in, draped with dead chickens, with cauliflowers on their heads, and huge baskets of eggs and cheese in their arms and almost in their teeth. There was no room for their merchandise on the floor so they just dumped it on the nearest passenger's lap and went out to fetch some more. We were all so exhausted by our sleepless night that none of us had the spirit to protest, and we could only sit and hope that it would not be for long. Fortunately, it was not. Two or three stations farther on, they all got out again.

We arrived late in Lemberg, and I had a frantic rush to catch my train, being hurled in by the porter as it was moving. I managed to buy three sandwiches and gave the rest of the money to the porter, so again I was facing a 24-hour journey with no money. But this time I was lucky, for there was nobody in the compartment but two women and a baby, and two young men. So I was able to curl up in a corner and go to sleep.

When I woke up I pulled out my bag of nuts and what remained of my Persian bread. The rest of the people in the carriage were puzzled by seeing me eat such stuff and began asking me questions in German, which of course I did not understand. Then a woman spoke to me in French: "These young men want to know if you always live on nuts," she said.

"They are pistachio nuts; I brought them from Persia," I replied and promptly fell asleep again.

The next time I woke up I heard the French-speaking lady explaining who I was to another young man. He saw that I was awake and asked me: "Would you like some whisky?"

"No, thank you."

"A cigarette?"

"No, thank you."

"Well, what would you like?"

"Some chocolate, please."

"How extraordinary — how extraordinary," he repeated.

"Why?"

"I thought you must be a cow-girl."

I did not quite understand why cow-girls were assumed to like whisky and hate chocolate, but I guessed that it was my scarf and my divided skirt that made him think I was one. When at last we reached Vienna he took my bag for me and I carried his, which was much lighter, and we struggled with frequent rests to a hotel across the square.

Next morning I went to Cooks' to collect my mail and found a letter from Miles. He was arriving in Bad-Gastein in two days and I was to meet him there and go climbing. But that is his story and he has written it.

CHAPTER NINE
RUSSIA AGAIN

I CAME home to England to find that my uncle and aunt had died within a week of each other and, as neither of them had made wills, their money came to my two brothers and me. I had already found how cheaply I could travel, for the whole journey from Meerut to London cost me less than £50. This legacy money completed my new independence. So long as I took my time about it I could now satisfy my craving to see the world, and I now knew that I could do so for less than it would cost me to live in England — which I thought was a dreadful idea anyway. Indeed, I found that the whole of my Chinese journey, described later in this book, was to cost me only £30.

I made all sorts of plans and, looking at maps of the vast land mass of Asia, I thought what fun it would be to go overland from Canton to Calais. I had done a large part already, but I still had to cover the ground from China to India.

All these plans had to be postponed for a year or so while we sorted out my uncle and aunt's estate, and I went through the horrid, sordid business of divorce. Meanwhile, I kept planning for the big journey. I thought it would be useful to learn German. I had so enjoyed my trip through Russia and was longing to see more of the country and to talk to the people, but I knew that I should never manage to learn Russian, least of all from books or formal lessons. The only way I can learn a language is by talking — I love talking. The Russians in the trains never seemed to find any difficulty in producing someone who spoke German, and I felt sure that if I went and lived with a German-speaking family who knew no English, I should soon pick up enough German to make myself understood in Russia.

Some friends put me in touch with an Austrian family living in Vienna. I bought a Baby Austin delivery van, which had only one seat so there was plenty of room for me to sleep in the back, and after a few weeks I was driving across France and Germany on my way to Vienna. While I was going through Germany I bought a camera, for now that I intended to spend my time travelling it seemed a pity not to have a good one. But even with the good camera that I bought, I never enjoyed taking photographs. Later, when I was enjoying myself with delightful people in lovely, photogenic surroundings in China or Japan, the voice of duty would say, "Now you must take a photo of this." Out would come the camera and at once everyone was self-conscious. The harmony was ruined and the spell quite broken.

After three months in Austria I could speak bad German and could understand it well enough, even if it was spoken fairly fast, though I could not read a word. I motored back to England, and in between visits to solicitors made other short dashes to the continent. Then, one day in the summer of 1936 I was staying with my brother, Charles Boxer, in Dorset when he received the news that he had been posted to Hong Kong and that he was to travel overland on the Trans-Siberian Railway to take up his appointment as intelligence officer there.

"Why don't you come too?" he said.

This was the chance that I had been waiting for. But as he was not going to stop in Russia longer than he could help, I decided to go on ahead and join him in Moscow. I left England three months before we were to meet in Moscow, for I was going to do some climbing in Austria and then stay with Leo and Erni Petrin, my friends in Vienna, before taking the train to Leningrad.

Erni was thrilled to hear that I was going to make a journey into Russia and persuaded me to buy a good, thick Loden coat. These coats are made of waterproof felt, usually in green or off-white. She took me to a small tailor who made coats for the big shops, and I bought an off-white Loden coat with a hood, interlined with wool, and lined and piped with dark-green tartan. I also bought what I thought were a very smart pair of green shoes with completely square toes. They made my feet look enormous.

While I was in Vienna I met a young newspaper reporter on the *Wiener Freie Presse*. His mother was an Austrian Jewess who had married a Russian, and during the Revolution they had escaped from Russia. His father had gone to the east and his mother to the west. She had taken their four young children, the youngest only six months old. The son, who was now grown up, had written a book, not yet published, about his mother's flight with the children in which he detailed all the horrors of the Revolution.

"Will you pass through Harbin?" he asked me.

"Yes."

"Then perhaps you could take the Russian translation of my book to my father. He still lives in Harbin, for he has no passport and cannot leave."

"Certainly," I replied, in a blaze of indignation at bureaucratic restrictions which could keep a family split up at opposite ends of the earth, and without thinking of the risks that I was letting myself in for. Charles would be travelling first class, and on the railway journey with him I would have to go first class too, but when I was on my own I was determined to travel third as I had done before. I fixed myself up with the necessary visas and third-class tickets from Vienna to Leningrad and on to Moscow, and first-class tickets from Moscow to Tokyo, where we were going to spend Christmas with the Dutch minister, a friend of Charles's. Then early one morning in October 1936 I got on the train for Warsaw. It was not very crowded; there was nobody else in the compartment except an elderly couple, the wife practically helpless with crying. Her husband was trying to comfort her and talk to a young couple on the platform, with the wife also in tears. At last, to everybody's relief, the whistle blew and we left.

I wanted to help the husband. He was such a small man, and his wife was taller and much fatter than he was, so that he could not get his arm round her to give her a hug; he could only give her little pats and hold her hand. He saw me watching him and started to apologize. When I answered in German, my dreadful accent brought the first ray of sunshine into his wife's day. We went on talking until she gradually stopped crying, and at the end of one of my very involved sentences she actually laughed.

We had one great thing to talk about, the fact that we were all three going to Russia. They were emigrating there to join their son, who was a Communist and had found it best to leave Austria where work was hard to find and Communists unpopular. He had got himself a good job in Russia, was able to write to them regularly, and had even come to Austria to visit them. They kept repeating that when he came he had two black suits, and this seemed to them to prove that in Russia there was a good standard of living. The father had lost his job, and he and his wife had to live with the married daughter and her husband; they were the couple who had been seeing them off. This arrangement had not worked out well. The old couple could not bear to be beholden to the son-in-law for every bite they took, and then the son in Russia had written and said that the father could easily get a job in Stalingrad where he was working. He said that if they could reach the Russian frontier, he would send them some money for them to collect there, together with the tickets for the rest of the journey.

It all seemed most odd to me, for during my brief journey through Russia the people had never seemed to me better off than the Austrians, and I could hardly believe that the son would really be able to come up all the way from Stalingrad to Moscow to meet his parents. But this was no time to tell them that. Everything they had in the world was with them on the train. All their other possessions had been sold to pay for the tickets to the frontier, and they could not turn back. They must have both been nearly 60, and there was no job for them in Austria. I did not tell them I had already visited Russia, for I could not have borne to answer the questions I knew they were sure to ask.

As soon as we crossed the frontier into Poland the carriage became jammed with peasants going to market. I was also surprised to see quite a lot of Jews, young and old, with long ringlets hanging down each cheek, and it struck me again how much that is typical of national life can be seen on a train, particularly in the cheapest class. First-class travellers all over the world are very much the same, only the language changes.

At Warsaw I hopped out of the train ahead of the Austrian couple — for I had much less luggage than they did — and started to find out when the train for Russia left and from which platform. I discovered that we had an hour to wait, so I went back to see how they were getting on. It was the first time they had ever been outside Austria, and they were quite bewildered by all the noise and the foreign language. They were delighted to see me, and I took them off to have a cup of coffee. They could not get over the way I had been able to find out the time of a train and order a cup of coffee in a strange land. I realized suddenly how much I had learnt, imperceptibly and happily, since I had left India on my own.

The train to Russia was naturally almost empty, and we three had a compartment to ourselves. The few other passengers left at intermediate stations, and there were hardly half a dozen other people on the whole train by the time we found ourselves crossing a kind of no-man's-land between the Polish frontier post and the Russian border. Perhaps it was my imagination but the landscape seemed to grow bleaker and bleaker as the train chugged indifferently along towards Russia until we came to a rather battered-looking archway with a painting of workers casting off enormous chains. Soon afterwards the train drew into the first Russian station.

By now it was five o'clock on a cold and windy evening. The station was shabby and bleak, with cracked cement, and a few men in uniform stood on the platform. We climbed out of the train and waited uncertainly for our baggage. Nobody took any notice of us, but we saw a few other passengers standing together at the other end of the train, so we joined them. I noticed some *guichets* with Russian writing over them and was relieved to see "Intourist" over one of them. There we found a woman who spoke German, and at once the Austrians broke into smiles and produced their son's letter and, I think, some sort of receipt to prove that he had sent off the money to them at the frontier. I left them to sort things out and carried my bag a bit nervously over to the table where the Customs were checking the baggage. The manuscript I had so lightheartedly accepted now began to make me feel uncomfortably panicky. I had just put it undisguised in my suitcase, for it was far too bulky to tie round my waist or put in my shoes. I had thought that the honest look and straightforward approach would be best. But now, with a gimlet-eyed Russian Customs man snapping questions at me, it was with sweaty hands and a furtive manner that I began to open my case. Luckily at this moment the Intourist woman appeared at my elbow.

"Come with me," she said.

"I must pass the Customs first," I replied quickly.

Then, as I hoped, she spoke to the Customs man, and he chalked my case and passed it back to me.

"The money for these Austrians has not arrived," she told me. "The wife is in tears and the husband thinks that perhaps you can comfort her."

She was friendly and obviously much worried about the old couple.

"The money has been sent," she kept repeating, "but it just has not arrived."

In the office the poor old lady was crying even harder than when she left Vienna, and I could not blame her, for I felt sure that things were even worse than she suspected. This was only the start; tomorrow she would find that her son had not been able to reach Moscow in time to meet them. I tried not to think what would happen after that. Her husband looked anxiously to me for help, and as I knew only one way of cheering her up, I set to and gave her a good earful of my ludicrous German. She had to stop crying and concentrate on me in order to understand, and that in itself was a good thing. There was nothing much I could tell them; they had no choice; they could only go on. Their Austrian money was finished, and all they had in the world were their tickets to Moscow and four smallish suitcases. There was nothing more to be done at the frontier station, so we all went along to the Russian train, with its big, shabby carriages, and soon we were moving on again through the same flat and depressing landscape.

With my railway tickets I had been supplied with meal-tickets which entitled me to third-class meals anywhere, though I never quite understood how they worked. Our train would split at two o'clock in the morning and I should have to leave the old couple and move into the part going to Leningrad. I thought it would be a good idea if I could give them a meal before I did so, for if the son did not turn up at Moscow it might be a long time before they got another. First of all I went to the restaurant-car and made sure that they would accept the tickets. All this bargaining was done in German, and I was very thankful that I had learnt it, for it had already proved extremely useful and made my journey much more interesting.

I thought that the meal in the restaurant-car would be pretty gloomy, but it turned out just the opposite. The old lady had never had a meal on a train before and was absolutely delighted with the faded Tsarist splendour all around her. I ordered vodka, and by one in the morning we were all three as happy as clams, as we rolled back along the rocking train to their compartment, where I said a very hasty good-bye and rushed off to the Leningrad section of the train before they fully realized what I was doing.

I never heard another word from them and have no idea what happened. Even if their son did meet them, things can hardly have turned out well for they would probably have been in Stalingrad during the war.

Leningrad in October seemed grey, drab and enormous. I was the only visitor in the hotel, and after doing my duty tour with Intourist in the morning, would spend the afternoons walking. The big wide streets, built to carry so much traffic, looked forlorn, with only hurrying pedestrians and an occasional droshky. I did see some cars but they were so rare that they were quite a phenomenon. I was surprised at the Hermitage and the other palaces. They still had many of the original pictures and furnishings, which looked in good condition too, though in the cold, grey, depressing weather among the shabby figures of the Russian sightseers it was sad work going round them.

As I walked about the streets in my new Loden coat, warm boots and gloves, people would every now and then come up and walk close behind me and mutter something to me. They seemed to be repeating the same words over and over again. At first I thought the men were trying to pick me up, but when a couple of women did the same thing I was quite baffled. They did not touch me; they just walked along beside and not quite abreast of me, muttering for two or three minutes, and then went off. Sometimes I pretended not to notice, sometimes I spoke in English or German, but it always ended the same way.

I had no Russian money and depended on the tickets for meals and drinks. There seemed little point in changing my money at a ridiculous rate of exchange; that would make everything far too expensive, even if there had been anything to buy. I noticed no shops that sold anything but food, and even they had long queues outside them and precious little inside.

One day I thought I would go to a cinema, so I changed some money and then went to a cinema where I had seen a long queue. I tailed onto the end of it, and soon I noticed that the people ahead of me went straight out into the street again after they had bought their tickets. At the ticket office I tried my German again, with great success.

"You can buy your ticket now," the woman told me, "but it will be for the next performance which does not start till half-past three."

As it was only two o'clock, I went into a café to sit down and keep warm. The people were not nearly as friendly as they had been in the south — nor had I made any friends in the train. After a while I grew tired of being stared at in the café, so I went out and walked again until it was time for the cinema.

The crowd outside was now immense, and a few minutes after I arrived I was completely hemmed in. By the time the people inside started coming out, I could not even move my arms, though, as I am tall, I could see what was going on. The crowd made no effort to get inside while the previous house was still coming out, but there was a solid surge as the last figure appeared.

I knew I had a ticket for the balcony and was wondering how on earth to get up there, as I swept in with the crowd, when I saw a curving stair on my right. Luckily the body in front of me seemed to be going that way too. I could not tell from the back what its sex was, for though the men were usually better dressed than the women, both were so muffled up in such various wrappings, and jammed together as we were it was pretty well impossible to see whether there were trousers or a skirt underneath it all. I gripped hold of the back of the coat, and we fought our way to the foot of the stairs. There we were engulfed by the rest of the balcony-ticket holders, and the pressure round me was so great that I was gradually forced off the ground and finally arrived at the top of the steps without my feet having touched a single one of them.

After all this tremendous effort, it turned out that the struggle was quite unnecessary. Not only were all the seats numbered, but the crowd, who had pushed and fought and struggled up the stairs, now waited docilely while one young girl looked at each ticket in turn and pointed out the seat.

The main film was a picture about the Spanish Civil War, and I was touched to see the audience so completely absorbed in the sufferings of the Spanish. Their own lives must have been a daily struggle and in a much more severe climate, yet they were heart and soul with the Spanish Republicans. The photography was splendid, with some wonderful close-ups of men fighting, and the emotional atmosphere was most infectious. I was almost sobbing myself, and the final scene when we watched the ragged smiling men marching towards Barcelona brought me to my feet with the rest, and cheering too.

Leningrad seemed to be haunted by ghosts of the old régime. The city had been laid out for plenty of rich and fashionable carriages, and the houses cried out for well-dressed people and liveried footmen standing in the doorways. But now the wide roads seemed empty, with the shabby people always slinking along by the walls. I was glad that my stay in Leningrad was short and that most of my time would be spent in Moscow.

I travelled to Moscow on an overnight train, and the other people in the carriage were nervous of me rather than actually hostile. I found one woman who talked German fluently.

"How do you come to speak German so well?" I asked her.

"I am a Jewess," she replied, and, with a reflex action acquired in Austria, I looked nervously round to see if anyone had understood her.

"Most of us Jews know German," she went on, smiling, "and since the Revolution we have never been discriminated against, so now quite a few Jews come here from other countries to enjoy some genuine equality."

This point of view fascinated me, and I would have liked to hear more, but she got out at the next stop, and none of the other passengers showed any signs of friendliness. Perhaps the recent purges had something to do with it, or maybe the northerners were naturally less friendly than the southerners.

Moscow itself seemed gay and exciting after Leningrad. There were quite a few cars on the road, and the people looked more brisk and hopeful. The hotel was crowded, which was a pleasant change, and the tours so busy that they must have been a strain on the guides. We went to hospitals, factories, and a People's Court. The judge entertained us to tea afterwards. The accused all stood up in turn and blithely admitted they were guilty and had been mistaken; they did not look at all upset or as if they were in fear. The court was packed with spectators.

In the hotel I was very pleased to find an American Baptist missionary on his way to China. His name was Johnson Mead and he was leaving for China on the same train as I was. He told me of places I ought to see in China and said he had friends who would help me, and we planned to spend some of the seven days on the train in choosing an interesting route to the Burmese border. In the meantime we concentrated on sightseeing in Moscow.

One of the things Johnson wanted to see was the memorial, somewhere on the walls of the Kremlin, which included the name of Reed, an American with whom he had been at college in the States and who had died fighting for the Bolsheviks. I think he half hoped he might get special treatment for being a college friend of one of the Heroes of the Revolution. But when we went to look for the memorial the sentries were most suspicious and eventually became quite threatening when we tried to explain the reason for our interest in the Kremlin wall.

We also went to the ballet and to several theatres, but by far the most interesting place we visited was a church. It was packed, and not only with old people as I had been expecting; many of the congregation were between 20 and 30. Most of them were women, and there were plenty of mothers with young babies. The priests' robes were of good stuff and beautifully embroidered, and the icons and vessels used for the service were all silver or gold, but the priests themselves looked very thin and frail. The sincerity of everyone there impressed me, although there was a rather feverish and hectic atmosphere about the service. The people had come in such crowds that we could hardly move, yet they did not seem to be finding the peace they were looking for. The congregation did not seem to merge in a common experience but everybody remained in their separate selves.

A friend of mine had written to a Belgian doctor who was living in Moscow working for the Russians, and one afternoon he arrived in my room at the hotel. He was a remarkable sight in a beret and riding boots.

"For the mud," he explained. "My room is in an area of new buildings. The houses were finished before the roads, and until the frost becomes permanent the mud is knee-deep."

He was very pleased with his research job. "It is wonderful. I only have to ask for what I want and I get it. They do not mind the expense. Special equipment from America or Germany; it is all the same to them. I just speak to them and tell them I must have this or that and within a week or two I have it. I do not even have to explain why I want it or to fill up any forms. It is wonderful."

"It sounds it," I said, "but surely there are some snags?"

"Yes, there is one," he replied. "It is very difficult to get foreign currency so that I can go out of Russia for my holidays."

He offered to take me to see the collection of Impressionist paintings in the Museum of Modern Western Art, and we went out to the nearest tram stop. As usual it was surrounded by a small crowd. The doctor was stockily built and was made almost spherical by his winter clothes. His top coat was fastened round his waist with a stout leather belt.

"Catch hold of my belt when the tram comes in," he said, "hold it with both hands and don't let go whatever happens."

I stood directly behind him while we waited, and as soon as the tram appeared I caught hold of his belt. My experience at the Leningrad cinema passed through my mind. The tram itself was already festooned with people hanging on outside, and none of them got off, at least as far as I was able to see, for I had no time to take in much as my doctor was already charging the tram. We were both better fed and considerably heavier than anyone else, and our combined weight moved a swath through the crowd and we arrived fairly easily on the platform. One quick-witted man had seized me by the waist and so managed to reach the platform in our wake. He penetrated no further, but as we were foreigners the passengers made an effort to let us go in and push our way to the other end. Inside it was suffocating and smelly but better than in the biting wind outside. Some Russians, I was convinced, spent their days inside the trams. The crowd was so dense it was impossible for the conductor to pass through and collect the fares. Passengers were only allowed to get off from the front of the tram, and for the whole of our journey the doctor fought his way up the length of the tram. It seemed to take a long time to me, and we had only just arrived on the front platform when we had to get off. That was easy. We found ourselves outside a large, dilapidated building with a dismal patch of garden in front, a muddy path, and acres of dirty snow. Several shabby figures were also going in.

There could have been no better prelude to seeing the paintings. They were like a revelation. All the light, gaiety and colour, so utterly lacking outside, were there. I felt we should all be dancing and singing, but after a while I calmed down a bit and began to look at the other people. There were far more than there would have been at any permanent collection in England. They looked very serious, or even puzzled, and I could not be at all sure they really liked the pictures. When we left I was delighted to see the proletariat all tipping the cloakroom attendant. When we were with Intourist guides anybody seen trying to tip was always told patronizingly, "There is no tipping in the Soviet Union. Everybody is well paid and has no need of tips."

After we had seen the pictures we started walking back, for I wanted to see as much of Moscow as I could, and I enjoyed walking and talking with someone who would answer my questions honestly. I had not had much opportunity of walking in Moscow except in the centre of the city, and now as we went along I suddenly heard again the muttered question I had so often heard in Leningrad. There was a man walking just behind me, six inches from my elbow.

"What on earth does he want?" I asked the doctor. "This was happening all the time in Leningrad, but today is the first time in Moscow."

The man beside me stopped muttering as soon as I spoke, but as soon as I had finished he began again.

"He is trying to buy your coat," the doctor explained. "They always do, if you are not with the Intourist. It is fantastic what you can get for clothes. That is the only way tourists can obtain roubles at a reasonable rate of exchange, by selling their clothes."

When I had first arrived at the Moscow Hotel they had taken my passport with my ticket for the Trans-Siberian train. This is what they always did, so I had not been worried, but now that I was leaving the next day I went to the office to find out if everything was ready. The girl in the office looked very alarmed when I told her my name. She disappeared into an inner sanctum and came out with a man, obviously an executive. He had my passport in his hand.

"I am sorry," he said. "It is, I know, our fault, but you have the wrong visa on your passport. It is for an exit on the west of Russia, and your ticket is for the east."

"Well, what happens now?" I asked. "My brother will be on the train tomorrow and I want to travel with him."

He shook his head sadly. "You cannot leave without the right visa, and we cannot get the right one in less than a week because all the offices are closed for the October Revolution celebrations. By next week you will have the visa and we will let you stay on in the hotel at no extra cost."

For a moment I was so angry that I could not speak. To wait a week and then to have to travel first class all by myself, with only other foreigners to talk to, was a miserable prospect. They would probably be mostly men, and seven days of isolation in the first class would be sure to cause trying complications.

Just then Miss Connelly, an economist I had met in the hotel who was writing a book on Russia, came up.

"What shall I do?" I asked her. "They want me to stay on another week because the visa on my passport is wrong."

"Of course you must go," she replied indignantly. "It's absurd to let them get away with it; they have plenty of time to telegraph the permission before you ever get to the frontier."

She turned back to the desk with me. The man and woman were still standing there, and I became very haughty now that I had strong reinforcements.

"You should have done it when I first gave you the passport. I cannot read Russian, so I could not tell it was wrong. My brother is expecting me, and I do not like to travel alone all that way. I will leave tomorrow as arranged and you can telegraph the permission direct to the frontier. The train does not get there for seven days, so there is plenty of time."

They looked at one another in horror and consternation.

"But we cannot do that. In Russia it takes far longer than seven days for a telegram to go so far, and if they send you back, you will have overstayed your time-limit and will have to go to prison."

I must have looked a bit shaken by this prospect, but a voice just beside me said, "Be firm, it's the only thing they understand. I have friends at the British Embassy and will go and see them in the morning and get them to be sure that the telegram goes off."

So I decided to be firm and said I would leave in the morning anyway.

"You must leave early," the girl said. "They are closing some of the main streets for the procession and the taxi will have to go a long way round."

Next morning I came down in plenty of time. Johnson was already there and we went to the counter together to collect our passports. The same girl was there again. She gave Johnson his passport first, and when I held out my hand she seized it in both of hers.

"Oh, don't go, please don't go!" she said, almost sobbing. "The telegram will not arrive and they will put you in prison."

"Please don't worry," I said. "Miss Connelly is asking the Embassy to help. I am sure it will be all right."

But she put no more faith in my words than I did myself, and when I turned round at the doorway I saw that she was weeping into her handkerchief.

The train was already in the station when we got there, and I soon found Charles. He had a compartment to himself and mine was next door, separated only by a washroom. Although I was so pleased to see him, I felt a bit sad when Johnson went off to his third-class carriage — that was my proper place, I thought. But I had other things to think of when the attendant who had taken my passport brought it back at once and said that the exit visa was wrong.

"It is quite all right," I replied airily, "just a mistake of the Intourist, and they are telegraphing the frontier."

To my relief, the attendant looked quite impressed and let it go at that.

I did not really enjoy the journey very much. In the big international Wagons-Lits there were very few passengers and none of them were Russian. The attendants were obsequious, and the only indication that we were in Russia was the view out of the window. It was gloriously Russian, with deep snow, immense distances and endless forests. If it had not been for Johnson in the third class, I would have had no contact at all with Russian people.

Each day I went along the train to see him in the third class. The idea at first had been that we should talk about my journey through China, but after the first day I found a family in his carriage who spoke German, and from then on we were so busy hearing about their life that we had hardly any time to discuss China.

I had always been interested in Russia and very fond of Russian literature, and now I was meeting people who had actually lived through experiences that might have come out of *And Quiet Flows the Don*.

The mother of the family was a qualified engineer who, at the age of 16, had been imprisoned in the Peter Paul Fortress in Leningrad. She had fought as a soldier in the Revolution and was a member of the Communist Party. Now she had been posted as an engineer to one of the new factories being built in Tomsk where, she said, they would be safe from German attack. With her were her three children, all in their teens. Her husband was not a party member, and he was not being transferred to Tomsk. She was a bit evasive about this part of the story, and I was not quite sure whether the authorities had refused him a transfer because he was not a party member or whether she had broken with him for the same reason. She said several times, "He does not want to be a party member."

Sometimes in the stations I would look out of the window and see prisoners, great gangs of them, squatting on their hunkers in the snow. It made me feel wretched to look at them. The sight of these prisoners and the tales I had been told by the family in the third class made me feel none too light-hearted about my improper visa as we approached the frontier of Manchukuo, which was being run by the Japanese who had installed Pu Yi, the last of the Mandarin dynasty, as their puppet emperor. I felt a moment's panic when I was woken by the Russian frontier officials at half-past two in the morning. Luckily they were much more interested in Charles, who was an officer, and I was merely dealt with by an underling. Perhaps he could not read; at all events he opened the passport at the right place, steadily regarded the wrong visa, and then gave it back to me and left.

CHAPTER TEN
ON FOOT IN JAPAN

THE Manchukuo train was all specklessly clean, polished and shining, with little spick-and-span attendants running to and fro. I hated it. Russia seemed so cozy and friendly by comparison, and as Johnson had gone on another train to China, I now had no excuse to visit the third class.

The carriages were all equipped with hot and cold running water that actually ran and really was hot. The fittings had been made to suit the Japanese figure and their position was mathematically calculated, so that when I washed my teeth and bent over the basin to spit, my bottom hit a shelf on the wall and I nearly knocked myself out in the basin. I put on the clean kimono that the railway company provided for one to sleep in, and of course both it and the bunk were far too short. I curled up and fell asleep quite soon, but almost at once I was woken up by a sudden slap on the behind. I clutched at the kimono and sat up, furious, to find a Japanese soldier shouting at me. He was armed with a rifle and wore a padded uniform and fur cap with ear-flaps. I pushed past him and went next door to tell Charles what I thought of the behaviour of Japanese soldiers. He went out into the corridor and asked the soldier what was the matter, and in no time they were chatting away like old friends. At last I could bear all this Japanese gossip no longer and interrupted.

"What does he want?" I asked.

"We are going through a military area, and he says we must stay in our compartments until they give us permission to leave and that we must keep the blinds down, otherwise we'll be arrested."

100

"That's no reason why he should slap me on the behind in the middle of the night."

"Oh, never mind," said Charles, equally, "he's a nice fellow and didn't mean anything."

At Harbin we stayed with the British Consul, and I told him I had a manuscript to deliver to a White Russian.

"Please do not let anybody see you leave the consulate to go to the White Russian sector," he said. "There is so much intrigue going on among the *émigrés*, they would be sure to jump to the conclusion that I am siding with one lot of them against another."

So I enjoyed myself walking all round Harbin, throwing off imaginary pursuers, before taking a droshky to the poor quarter where the White Russians lived. I had already found that when I travelled in the Orient among teeming millions of poverty-stricken people my sense of pity became — in sheer self-defence — rather blunted. And then suddenly this barrier of self-defence broke when I realized that there were white westerners living like the poorest of the Orientals and without any hope. These Russians had not a chance of managing to live as well as the Chinese would do on the same wages, and naturally the Chinese resented them coming and trying to take work away from the local people. The Russians had not come because they wanted to; they hated China and had not the least interest in the country or the people, and they were far too poor to have the leisure to try to interest themselves in their surroundings. They huddled together in the same buildings and quarrelled violently all the time. Nature carried on as usual, so the place was swarming with children.

My reporter friend's father was a surprise; tall, blond and blue eyed, he looked barely older than his son and, despite his gloomy surroundings, he seemed not to have a care in the world. He was living with a rather drab-looking woman, and I got the impression that it was she who did the work and provided for the family. I handed over the manuscript. He was delighted to have it and showed it proudly to the woman, but when he asked me to stay for tea, I could not bring myself to accept. The atmosphere was too overpowering, what with the smell, the air of utter hopelessness, and the almost continual sounds of people quarrelling and fighting.

The situation in Manchuria at this time was almost inextricably complicated. The Japanese and various factions of Chinese were all fighting one another, but there had been no official declaration of war and nobody seemed to know who was fighting against whom. When Charles and I arrived in Mukden we went to a hotel run by Japanese. It had all the Japanese amenities; there were free kimonos to sleep in, bedroom slippers and, best of all, handsome Japanese lavatories in which one crouched and hung on to a beautifully designed and very graceful porcelain pillar which ended in a swan's head.

We were only 24 hours in Mukden, during which time it was officially retaken for the umpteenth time. I think it was taken by the Chinese, but I am not sure. It all seemed very orderly, though there was supposed to have been some fighting, but in China, where somebody almost always finds an occasion to celebrate with fire-crackers, it is not so easy to pick out the sound of rifle-fire. Anyway, Charles and I stood at the hotel window and watched the victorious troops march in. The Japanese hotel staff watched too, and they seemed quite unmoved — perhaps with good reason, for I later learnt that the town was re-occupied by the Japanese a week later. The account in the newspapers sounded very dramatic. But whenever I find myself in a revolution or a war, I notice nothing. I have no eye for the dramatic.

We did a quick tour of some old tombs in heavy snow and then went down through Korea to Pusan where we took the ferry for Shimonoseki. The next day, when we arrived in Japan, the Japanese officials set upon poor Charles. They could not understand why he, a British Army officer of 30, was not going to stay at the British Embassy, as they would have expected, but with the Dutch minister, an old man in his 70s.

"This is most unusual," they said. "Why are you staying with this man?"

"He is a friend of mine," Charles replied.

But this simple and truthful answer seemed to throw them all into the greatest consternation. They were obviously convinced that he was a spy and searched every bit of his luggage until they nearly made us miss the train to Tokyo. When at last Charles forced himself out of their clutches and leapt into the already-moving train, he was followed by a little bespectacled shadow, who stood outside the carriage door and even followed him to the lavatory and watched that too.

The Japanese have an absolute mania for spies. Their history and legends are stuffed with spy stories, and it seems to be a sort of national weakness. Moreover they find it very difficult to believe the truth. When we were questioned we found it best to answer with a thumping lie. Even as we walked about the streets in Tokyo, plain-clothes policemen would suddenly materialize, showing their official badges and asking, "Name? Surname of Father and Mother? Age?" and so on. They wrote down our names phonetically in Japanese, and each policeman spelt them differently, so there was little chance that the official who received the reports would ever know that they all referred to the same people, especially as we would give different answers to different policemen. We would add ten years to our ages each time we were asked until we reached 100, and then we would go back to ten and start again. It prevented us from getting annoyed with the little men, and we enjoyed watching them earnestly writing away that our mother was Elizabeth Fry and our father James Watt, and that I was 90 and Charles 100. They were quite happy with these answers and some of them were even pathetically pleased that we were not angry with them.

But I felt that as long as I lived at the Dutch Legation and was so closely associated with Charles, who, as a Japanese-speaking army officer had such a high spy potential, I did not stand much chance of getting to know and like the Japanese. So I decided to go for a trip on my own instead of leaving for Hong Kong with Charles. In *Murray's Hand-Book to Japan for 1905* I found a description of an attractive walk across the island of Kyushu, ending up with a train journey to Nagasaki, where I could easily catch a boat for Hong Kong. So I went down to Kobe and took a small coasting steamer from there to Beppu on Kyushu.

It was very cold in Japan in January, and I was dressed in my white Loden coat, my green, square-toed shoes, and on my back was a mountaineering rucksack on a frame. As I came into the third-class ladies' compartment on the boat I must have looked enormous. It was already fairly full of women and children. They all gave a kind of gasp as I entered, and then after a moment of shocked silence all the children burst out screaming and rushed to their respective mothers, trying to hide from the fearful sight. It was a disconcerting start to the voyage; I had never been an object of terror before and I did not like it much.

The cabin was fairly roomy; its floor was covered with the clean matting the Japanese call *tatami*, and along each wall was a raised platform about eight inches from the floor. This was also covered with *tatami*, but it had some quilts laid out neatly to show the amount of space each passenger was allotted for sleeping, with our heads against the wall and our feet towards the centre of the room. I found a vacant quilt and quickly sat down, to make myself smaller and less frightening. The children stopped screaming and merely whimpered, and as I gradually took off my rucksack, coat and shoes, they became more and more curious about me and started peeping round from behind their mothers' kimonos.

It was stuffy in the cabin, for we seemed to be in the centre of the ship with no portholes, but it was miserable weather outside and I did not want to start another outburst of crying by standing up again, so I decided to wait till morning before exploring the ship. When the mothers had finished putting their children to bed, they gathered round me and we began to make friends with the help of a conversation book I had got from the tourist office. By next morning I was on good terms with the mothers and the children were quite accustomed to me. They were more inclined to laugh than to cry, but I cannot say that this was much less disconcerting.

We were going through the Inland Sea which, even in winter, looked perfectly lovely. Luckily it was a fine day. We passed thousands of little islands, some with a few snow patches and nearly all with the lovely, twisted trees that appear in so many Japanese prints. The little ports we stopped at were all like stage sets, and it was hard to believe that they were real and would still be there after we had sailed away.

By now my opinion of the Japanese was beginning to change a little and I was starting to enjoy myself. The meals on the boat were ghastly; I just managed to swallow enough to keep myself alive, for there was nothing at all to tempt the appetite. Thank goodness there was plenty of green tea for the asking, for I love it, and what with the tea and the scenery the journey went like a flash. The morning we reached Beppu I felt quite sorry.

By the time I had disembarked it was too late to start on my walk, so I spent the night at a terrible, European-style hotel. It was poky, sordid and boasted the dirtiest tablecloths I have ever seen and a five-foot bed of lumps. I was up at the crack of dawn to start walking.

The town was not large and I was soon in the outskirts, and then, a couple of miles along a motor road, I found the track described in *Murray's Hand-Book* of 32 years before. It led away into the hills and through occasional clumps of trees. The path went up and down and curled round rocks and boulders; there seemed to be no one about but me, and I was almost glad of the extra weight of my rucksack, as the wind was piercing. I had some food with me which I ate on the way, and it was lucky I had brought it for there was nowhere that I could buy any. The guide-book recommended a hotel where one should stay the night, but I had not expected the route there to be quite so desolate; all the country on this route between Beppu and Kumamotu was a jumble of mountains and streams. There had been several sharp showers; I was beginning to feel wet as well as cold and, with my usual perversity, after a glorious day spent by myself in beautiful surroundings, I was beginning to long for the hotel promised me by Murray.

At last I came to the village where the hotel was. It was perfect, better than anything I could have imagined. As I arrived at the door, the proprietor and his wife appeared, bowing and smiling. She gently touched my wet coat and, with a look of consternation on her face, started to undo the buttons. Two little maids came running up, one of them taking the wet coat with great expressions of sympathy, while the other took off my shoes and gave me a pair of warm, dry slippers. The other maid came hurrying back and the three women, making little cooing noises at me almost like doves, escorted me with affectionate little pats to my room.

It was enormous, and the *tatami* on the floor was thick and springy to walk on. There was an alcove with a *kakemono* hanging in it, and a flower arrangement underneath. We all left our slippers just outside the sliding door and, as soon as we were inside, two of the women started to undress me while the third went running off and came back in a few minutes with a small charcoal brazier and a pot of green tea. I was wrapped up in two kimonos, first a clean cotton one and then a big padded silk one, with a sash tied round my waist.

Then we all sat — at least I sat and they squatted neatly back on their heels — round the brazier, and we passed the conversation book back and forth at the chapter called "For the Hotel". When we tired of that, they unpacked my rucksack and exclaimed in delight or surprise at everything they found.

After a while I pointed to a phrase about the bath, and we all trooped off down a passage until we reached a room with a huge wooden tub with a charcoal fire underneath it and a smaller tub for washing in at the side. The proprietor's wife left me here, and the two little maids undressed me again and washed me, using the water from the smaller tub. They allowed me to step into the big tub by myself and I was nearly killed by the heat; it was so full of water that even when I sat bolt upright only my head stuck out. They produced an enormous towel which they warmed at the brazier and, as soon as I stepped out of the tub, they wrapped me up and rubbed me vigorously until I was thoroughly dry. We trooped back to my room again, and they made me comfortable on the floor with a kind of bolster to lean against while they trotted off to prepare my dinner.

I am not very fond of Japanese food, which puts far too much emphasis on appearance and not nearly enough on taste, but this dinner was so lovely and the little maids coaxed me so sweetly to eat it and looked so downcast when I did not seem to appreciate it, that in the end I thoroughly enjoyed every mouthful. When I had finished, they carried away the little lacquer table and small cooking brazier and busied themselves about making my bed. The whole of the room, except for the window, consisted of cupboards with sliding doors that made the walls of the room, and out of these cupboards they pulled countless quilts of various thicknesses. There were at least three heavy ones, three or four inches thick; they went on the floor for me to lie on, and another three or four thinner ones came on top. I prevailed on them, with some difficulty, to let me clean my teeth myself, and then they tucked me up in bed, opened the window a little, put the light out, and tiptoed quietly away.

The bed was so blissfully comfortable that I tried to stop myself falling asleep so that I could enjoy it consciously for longer. But I failed dismally.

Next morning I was woken up by the two little maids chirping round my bed. They brought me tea and dressed me in my own clothes which they had carefully dried. Then we all squatted round the little lacquer table for some rather indifferent breakfast, but again I could not resist their coaxing and managed to eat enough to keep them happy. When I left, the proprietor and his wife again appeared and stood at the door with the two maids, bowing and waving till a bend in the road carried me out of sight. I was in high spirits, the weather looked less rainy and the going was better, with a broader path and not so many trees; and as I was fairly high up there were good views.

At the first village I came to, there was great excitement; people came running out of their houses to look at me and then followed me along the road. Since tourists started using motor-cars I suppose foreigners have given up walking along Murray's path. The last house in the village was a school, and as I arrived all the children came running out, shouting and screaming. There was an instant hush when they saw me, and then they stood with their mouths agape in awed silence as I walked past. The parents who had been following me stayed at the school, and I soon heard the hum of comment. I met nobody upon the road, but after about an hour I was suddenly surprised to hear a bicycle bell behind me. I looked round and there was a boy of about 12 overtaking me. He passed by quickly, but I had time to see that he was wearing a bandage round his neck.

Soon the path became steeper, and I could see that I was coming to another village. When I reached the outskirts I heard a high call and saw the boy with the bandage round his neck jump down off a wall and run on ahead. Then came the sound of a bell, and when I rounded the next bend I found the schoolchildren all running out of school. Again there was the same silent staring and, after I had passed, the babel of comment. It was not till a couple of villages later, when two other cycling schoolboys had overtaken me on the road and I had twice heard the school-bell ringing and seen the schoolchildren run out as I entered the village, that I realized they must have been using me as a kind of object lesson. However, I was so pleased with Japanese hotels that I could not take exception to such a practical use of a tourist.

The rest of the path was much the same: little villages and dream-like hotels, always with two serving-maids. There are always two, as otherwise they are liable to get into difficulties with the male guests, and there were far too few females travelling alone to have established any different custom for dealing with them.

Close to the route, in the middle of the island, is Aso-san, a volcano much frequented by honeymooners and suicides. The weather was not good the morning I left to climb the volcano. The regular way up was by train or road from Kumamotu, but I was approaching it from the other side. The good track, which I had followed all the way from Beppu, did not lead to the top but went on to another village, so I had to be careful to find the right turning. It was a path to the right and would have been easy to find in clear weather.

This day it was raining and misty and with a wind that grew stronger the higher I climbed. I tried two right-hand turns before I found what I thought was the right one. It gave me an eerie feeling to walk alone along a narrow, twisting path on what was obviously the edge of a cliff and yet not be able to see anything but cloud all round. The track became rather faint and narrow, and I was thinking that I must have missed the proper path when I noticed that I was walking on volcanic ash; that meant I must be somewhere near my objective. I went slower and looked carefully at the ground. Gradually, I noticed footprints which became clearer as the ash grew thicker. Finally I was walking in deep ash, not really on a path at all, but just following the footprints ahead of me. They seemed to belong to a family, as there were two sets of adult footprints, one much larger than the other, which made me think they belonged to a man and wife. Then there were two or three sets of small ones that could have only belonged to children.

Every now and then a sudden puff of wind would bring a shocking, choking taste of sulphur. I began to speculate on this family, who must have ploughed their way through virgin ash for by now all signs of a path were gone and there were no returning footsteps. I climbed slowly higher and the choking sulphur blasts came more frequently. Now and then I heard a kind of groaning sigh, which, if it had not always been followed by an extra blast of sulphur, I would have been inclined to attribute to an underground god. I wrapped my mouth up in a scarf to stop coughing, for now I had been climbing so steeply that I could only breathe through my mouth. There came out of the mist a sudden, much louder groan, followed this time by a hot sulphuric blast that made me choke and my eyes fill with tears. I stopped a minute, uncertain what to do, and then looked at the footprints. They were still clear and going ahead into the mist so I followed them on, when suddenly there came an extra loud and powerful sigh and with a rush of hot sulphurous air the mist cleared a little so I was able to see that I was on the ragged brink, the very edge of a bubbling lake of pitch, and there the footsteps stopped. But there was no one there.

I felt a little sick. I did not want to think further. I knelt down to look closer and then saw there was one extra set of footprints and that they had turned back. I turned back too. I hurried down the way I had come up until I noticed one pair of footsteps leading away from the others on a track that I had not noticed on my way up. I followed them and in no time they led me out onto a small but distinct path, no doubt the one I should have been following all the time. This eventually brought me out at a flat parking place with kiosks and a tram-station.

In a small snack-bar I had some tea and a sandwich. The only other customers were a young Japanese couple: he was in European dress and hung with cameras, she wore Japanese dress, and both had mouths full of gold-decorated teeth. With an enormous gold smile the young man addressed me in pretty fair English and asked me my age, nationality and what I was doing. Then we sat down with a pot of tea.

"We go back to Kumamotu on tram in half an hour," he told me.

"Good," I replied. "I will come too."

"Have you seen Aso-san?"

"Yes."

"Only yesterday a whole family suicided in it," he said.

"How do you know?" I asked, the footprints in my mind.

"It was the father, he wrote a letter to say he had been passed over for promotion in office, and so he commit suicide, taking wife and three children, too."

The office manager had notified the police, and they had got in touch with the public works department, who had sent a man who knew the volcano well. He had found the footprints leading to the lake of pitch early that morning and had just got back with the news a couple of hours before me.

After this drama the ride down to Kumamotu seemed dull, but I was thankful to be in the tram at all.

"Where are you staying in Kumamotu?" the young Japanese asked me.

"I don't know yet," I replied. "A hotel in the Japanese style, I hope."

"Oh no, you must come to our hotel, it is most up-to-date, so European."

I stupidly allowed them to persuade me and, of course, it proved to be as horrible as I had feared, and I was thankful to go on to Nagasaki where I caught the boat for Hong Kong.

The boat looked smart enough and the first class was most elegant, but the third class, which I was in, was disastrous. Instead of being on Japanese lines like the boat from Kobe to Beppu, it was down-at-heel European. The cabins at night seethed with cockroaches, and the food consisted of a ghastly grey stew full of indeterminate lumps. I could not bring myself to eat enough of them to discover if they were meat or fish or merely wodges of rice.

These contrasts in the Japanese way of living from one place to the next set me against the country. The wonderful glossy first class, cleaned everywhere to hospital standards, and the sordid third class that I was in, where no one cleaned anything at all, the lovely Japanese-style hotels and the filthy, would-be European ones, the constant bowing and gold-toothed smiles, and the joy in drunkenness, all combined to make me feel that there was something unsound, schizophrenic perhaps, about Japan, as if the whole country was on the edge of a nervous breakdown.

I had thoroughly enjoyed my walk, only to find that it ended in that ghastly, senseless suicide. I always had the feeling that I had strayed onto a stage and that the players were all quite different people under their costumes, but that no matter how long I stayed there I would never know them except in their stage characters.

CHAPTER ELEVEN
FALLING IN LOVE WITH THE CHINESE

I T was a relief to arrive in Hong Kong. Charles was waiting for me on the quay, and we went off to his flat where he was already installed with two perfect Chinese servants in a typical bachelor establishment. I was immediately swept up into the social round which, apart from the scenery, was exactly the same as in India. I quite enjoyed it, but it was not what I had come so far to find and I was longing to get on into China itself.

I found a letter waiting for me from Johnson Mead. He said he had missionary friends in Changsha and they would like me to stay with them on my way to Ichang, and he advised me to find out before I started about the military and political situation in the country between Hong Kong and the Yangtze, as trouble sometimes flared up there and it might be awkward for me if I happened to be passing through at the time.

Everybody I met had different advice for my journey, and almost every meeting ended in an arrangement to meet again at cocktails or swimming so that I could be given some more advice by someone else. All this advice may have been well enough meant but it seemed intended to terrify me. It was no use my saying to myself that most of what I had been told about Persia — and above all the Persians — had proved hopelessly wrong. I began to feel that I could no longer trust my own feelings and experience, and I went on getting into more and more of a lather about it. I had been in Hong Kong for more than three weeks by the time I actually set off.

Leaving Hong Kong was a bit of a cheat because I went up to Canton second class and started the real journey from there. My first sight of the Chinese third class at Canton was a lovely surprise after the trains I had known in India. There was a corridor, which was splendid, the sexes were not segregated, and so all the children were not crammed into the female compartment; this in itself made me feel that I was up one class.

I arrived an hour before the train was supposed to start but it was already very crowded. Among my many other warnings in Hong Kong someone had said to me, "The Chinese are very hostile to anyone who does not belong to their family group. They are not helpful or friendly even to other Chinese; and for foreigners it is much worse."

This at once proved to be untrue. The Chinese in the carriage into which I was trying to force myself immediately set about fitting me in. They had already allotted themselves the space they thought they were entitled to, but I noticed that they were trying to give more room to me than to the only other person travelling alone.

My luggage was much more practical and more easily stowed than it had been on my Persian journey: just a rucksack and a Japanese *baifu*, a square piece of material tastefully decorated in a hand-painted design of green mountains on a dun background. I had replaced the heavy *poshteen* and blanket flea-bag by a light-weight eiderdown sleeping-bag and took only one pair of shoes. I also carried a certain amount of food: things like Horlicks tablets and dried fruit. It is no use my taking chocolate as an emergency ration because I have not the strength of mind to keep it till I need it.

We all squeezed down on the seats, but conversation was limited to bows and smiles. The rest of the time till the train left, people went on getting in and staying in; there was a constant noise of shouting, arguing and fighting, but I had already been in China long enough hardly to notice it unless it was addressed directly to me. Even so, I could not help noticing the crescendo of noise as the train started to move.

As we jogged through the fertile, neat countryside, and I knew I had started, my spirit lifted; I forgot all the gloomy warnings of robbery and rape, and I was filled with a special happiness that seems to come from completely cutting all ties. It was then that I fell in love with the Chinese, and I am still. There is a dignity and independence about them which is fascinating, but above all I love their practical common sense. They knew I could not talk to them and that it was probably a waste of time trying to explain, so if they wanted me to move my feet they simply lifted them up and held them firmly until they had adjusted the baggage underneath. Then they put the feet back in what they considered would be the most comfortable position.

They were constantly eating snacks, and eventually the time came for the main meal. This involved a major operation of baggage-shifting, so that all sorts of fascinating little pots and dishes could be brought out. But they did not offer me a taste of everything as the Persians had done.

I noticed only one other foreigner on the train, a small, dark man of unidentifiable nationality. He pushed his way through the corridor a couple of times and tried to be friendly to me, but I thought that it would look better to the Chinese if the foreigners did not immediately gang up together, so I pretended not to notice his advances.

There was not much we could do to make ourselves more comfortable for the night as we had already used up every available bit of space. Although I felt as if I were in a lemon-squeezer, I had more room than any other single Chinese, so after a few abortive blows on either side I resigned myself to a pretty sleepless night.

Next morning I was woken up by great goings-on. People were pushing around with smart enamel basins and mugs, and there was a great cleaning of teeth. We all stood up and stretched and rearranged ourselves, then, leaving my neighbours in charge of my baggage, I joined in the queue for the lavatory.

I managed to improve my frowzy appearance, but there was no hope of coming up to Chinese standards. They must be born uncrushable. I went back to my compartment and for breakfast sucked a Horlicks tablet and wished I had not relied on buying my food in the stations, which was rather more difficult here than it had been in India where I could speak the language and where there was not such a bewildering variety of food to choose from.

Then I saw my little foreigner pushing down the corridor again. He approached me with a beaming smile.

"I am Turk," he said, "and Turks do not like to eat alone. Please will you eat with me?"

He could not have come with a more welcome idea, and I followed him along to his compartment, where there was a bit more room. He gave me a terrific meal: chicken and rice and soup and cakes; and I liked him better with every bite I took. I asked him what he did and how he came to be in China.

"I am chemist, and I sell my pills all over China," he said, proudly pointing to several suitcases which were, I suppose, stuffed with his handiwork.

As I steadily worked my way through his lunch, he told me his history. He had somehow or other been an officer in the Russian Army, and when the Revolution came he found that the quickest way back to Turkey was through China. Then came the all-too-common story of those thousands of White Russian refugees. A fellow officer had asked him to make a detour to fetch his daughter who was still at school. They got to the school in time, but soon the father died, leaving the 16-year-old girl in the Turk's care. He looked at me gravely.

"I promise him," he said, "to take care of her and to protect her."

"How did you manage?"

"At first I look after her as a brother, then as an uncle, then as a cousin, then as a husband."

As we sat there, squeezed together, eating his good food and I listened to his story, I began quite to like him. When he offered to build me a house in Weihaiwei and look after me as a cousin, I felt almost complimented.

"But it would be difficult," I said. "What would your wife say?"

His eyes were full of tears when he turned to answer me, "She is dead, that is why I like you. You are like her, so large and so white."

Fortunately the train was getting near Changsha and I had to fight my way back to my own compartment.

In Changsha I was going to stay with Johnson's missionary friends. Whatever you feel about missionaries in foreign lands, there is no doubt that in China they were of the greatest help to travellers. We were not an absolute burden on them either, and they found us very useful for sending stuff that they did not like to trust to the post. If you live a life isolated from your own coun-trymen and from people of your own race, it feels rather like a landfall after a long time at sea when one of them turns up.

When I got out of the train I was very pleased with my first real contact with the Chinese. Admittedly, they had not been exuber-antly friendly, but they were far from standoffish or unhelpful. These were the Chinese who were accustomed to foreigners and who would therefore be more likely to be suspicious of them. I was looking forward to meeting others who lived farther inland and were less sophisticated.

A Chinese convert met me at the station and took me in a rickshaw to the mission which was some way outside the main town. It was an American mission and so was larger and far more comfortable than the English ones. Mr. and Mrs. Clark, who were running the mission, came out of the house to greet me. He was thin and anxious looking, a passionately sincere Christian. His wife was plump and jolly with a happy-go-lucky nature which, with her genuine goodness, probably made a much greater appeal to the Chinese than her husband's more serious approach. They knew what third-class travel was like and so they bustled me off to a hot bath in a tin tub. After that they gave me supper, at which I was introduced to peanut butter for the first time. Mrs. Clark made it herself and they used it instead of butter, which was almost unprocurable, for the Chinese do not eat it.

I was taken to see some famous ruins, but I have forgotten what they were. I am an ardent sightseer, but though I rarely miss a sight and I thoroughly enjoy seeing them, I do not find that I can remember them clearly for long. On the other hand I shall never forget the bicycle ride to the ruins. Speaking a foreign language and riding a bicycle are two things I can never learn to do; all the same I do them constantly and love it. Bicycling is the more alarming of the two; I have never been able to stand on the pedals and can only occasionally lift one hand from the handlebars while under way, but when they asked me if I could ride a bicycle, I firmly said, "Yes."

China is divided roughly by the Yangtze into the rice-eating and the noodle-eating halves. We were definitely in the rice half, and this meant that our way to the ruins was across the rice fields. They are separated by small banks about two feet high and looking from the seat of a bicycle as if they were six inches wide. These banks are neat and geometrical, with a smart right angle at each corner of the field. Of course, you do not hurt yourself much if you fall into a rice field, but I object to falling off on principle. The Clarks were very good on their bikes. I sweated heavily, with both hands clamped to the handlebars as I crept behind them. Each turn was agony, but with only a couple of falls I made our objective. All the time we were looking at the ruins I was thinking only of the ride back. No doubt this is why I can remember nothing about them. In time my bicycling over all kinds of tracks improved, but it never came up to missionary standards. They were all absolute masters of the art.

The next day I was back on the station to cram myself into the train for Wuchang. There we had to disembark from the train in order to cross the river on a ferry to Hankow. The scene at Wuchang station was dreadful. It had been a tiring journey, and then we were catapulted into the middle of ravening wolves disguised as Chinese coolies. It was bitterly cold with grey skies, dismal rain, and no shelter from the weather or from the huge, dense crowd of underfed coolies — there were at least three to every train passenger. I could carry all my baggage myself, but it seemed safer to get a coolie, even if only to protect me from the rest. The difficulty was to choose. They seized hold of my coat, shrieking and screaming and thrusting their unblown noses right into my face in an endeavour to be chosen. I tried to use a few words of what I hoped was Chinese to make them understand how much I was prepared to pay. I think they must have understood, for a perfect howl of anguish went up when I gave out the amount. So I raised my price a bit, picked a coolie wildly at random, and pushed my things at him.

Immediately peace fell, and I walked quietly and amicably with him onto the ferry. Indeed he turned out to be a charming man who took a lot of trouble to find me a nice, dry place. When I gave him what I had promised, he thanked me and moved off with no argument at all. This came as a wonderful surprise after what I had been used to with Indian coolies. They would have had a wailing story about poor relations and dozens of children; on the other hand, there would not have been the original terrible scene. This was no isolated incident: I found that it was the way things were done in China; once the agreement had been reached, you were allies.

Now that I had reached Hankow, the next thing to do was to go up the Yangtze. As soon as I started to make inquiries I was given the gloomiest warnings: it was the wrong time of year, the water was too low, and so on and so on. This turned out to be good news for me. With the water low, the European steamers would not run, for the insurance would not cover them, so I had to travel Chinese. This was much cheaper; all I had to do was to get on the boat.

I found out which day the boat started, but I had no idea of the time it left, so I rushed off in a panic early in the morning and found that there were already quite a few passengers on board. My third-class ticket gave me the right of a bunk on a sort of scaffolding erected below decks. It was an enormous place and slept well over a hundred. The shelves where we slept were in three tiers round the walls, and there was a perfect maze of them in the middle, with alley-ways to the doors. Luckily, I got a top tier on the wall, with my head next to one Chinese's feet and my feet next to another's head.

The steamer did not leave till midday, and it seemed that they did not usually start until they were full up. Although the weather was cold and misty most of the time, it was a delightful trip. We spent a week twisting and turning with the Yangtze. There was not much we could see over the banks, as the water was so low, but across the flat, brown water, with figures in blue on the bank outlined against the lovely sky, every piece of cultivated land looked like a picture. I was half-hypnotized. The days slipped by; there was something to do all the time, and yet the view, though changing as you watched it, seemed almost to recur again and again.

What I enjoyed most was being with the Chinese. I was the only foreigner on board. They took a great interest in me and absolutely won my heart by their genuine admiration for my "dressing-gown for third-class Occidental ladies in the Orient". I had designed it specially for myself and made it up out of a piece of kimono cloth that I had bought in Japan for the purpose. It was brightly coloured, with an interesting design of pheasants on bamboos that I hoped might help in conversations about the local birds, and it was built rather like a tent with a hole in the top for my head. There was plenty of room inside for me to change my clothes completely, and I had given it fairly large armholes with long, full sleeves so that even when I was using it to change in public, I could still shake hands with strangers or take a cup of tea.

The first day they were barely friendly and that night when I went to bed I thought it best not to change in the corridor below the bunks in case I would be in the way. So I retreated to my upper bunk and started changing there. As it was pretty narrow and there was not enough room to sit upright, I had to thrash about a good deal before I could appear in my pyjamas. All this naturally attracted the attention of my near neighbours, and when I made my debut — hot, dishevelled, but completely changed — one of them ran off to fetch his wife. When he came back with her he seized my gown and put it on himself to show her how useful it was.

Next morning they were much more friendly, but in some indefinable way I knew as I finished my dressing that there was something wrong. The matter was not cleared up until there had been a certain amount of argument among my fellow-passengers. Then the man on the next part of the upper tier to me, whose head I had remorselessly pushed all night with my feet, came round to me with an enamel basin decorated with large red roses and full of nearly boiling water, a huge tooth-mug, and a towel with "Good Morning" embroidered on it in English. He gave a demonstration of washing his face and teeth, and they all made it clear that it was a poor show on my part that I had not provided myself with a basin and mug. They took a kinder view of me when I brought out my towel, toothbrush and soap. Each morning after that, as soon as my neighbour had finished washing, he brought me his basin and mug filled with hot water.

After dressing was over, we had our breakfast of hot noodles and tea, the meals being included in the price of the fare. Then came the time for the lavatory. It was rather like a bird-cage and hung out over the stern. There were two, side by side, and the part you entered from the boat was made of wood, with a wooden door, while the rest consisted entirely of iron bars, so you could see your neighbour at his morning duty but the people on the boat could not see either of you. The bars on the floor were four or five inches apart, and underneath ran the mighty Yangtze — which was simple, practical and reasonably hygienic.

It seemed no time at all before we were called for lunch. This was an excellent meal with as much food as you could eat and lots of variety. We had to use chopsticks and I already had some of my own. Wooden chopsticks were provided on the boat but they were not very strong and sometimes had splinters; I noticed that most of my table-mates used their own. At first I was very slow and I missed some of the best dishes because I could not manage to reach across the table, pick out what I wanted, and carry it all the way back to my mouth. As soon as the Chinese realized why I did not take certain dishes, they very kindly helped me. They did not pass the dish to me but used their chopsticks to put the food on my plate or even straight into my mouth. If they had not all had such wonderful teeth I would have been hard put to swallow some of the food I received in this way. We had as much rice as we could eat and some people stowed away the most tremendous amounts. At first I could only manage one bowlful, but by the time we reached Ichang I could easily manage two and a half. We finished by passing round the boiling water. We took a good swig of it, rinsed out all the particles of rice sticking to our teeth, then spat it out. It made your mouth feel very nice and fresh, and there is no better way of getting rid of the grains of rice.

I had some knitting with me and also a few books. The Chinese did not read much but they played Mah Jong and finger-games and were always drinking tea. One elderly man spent nearly the whole journey ambling up and down the deck, taking little sips of tea from the spout of a tiny teapot.

We ate our evening meal, which was pretty much the same as the lunch, at about five o'clock, and somehow by eight-thirty I was quite ready for bed. Each night I put on my dressing-gown and changed under it into my pyjamas, with never less than 50 people watching me. When I was ready they would help me up into my bunk and, although I had a sleeping-bag, they would carefully go through the motions of tucking me in.

The atmosphere was curiously unreal all the time I was on the boat. I felt that I was not really there and that the cormorant-fishers' boats which we passed so regularly — with a man in blue, motionless in the stern, and the cormorants sitting staring fixedly at the water — might just have been one boat filing past us again and again. I began to feel that we were not moving but just watching scenery as it passed by us. So it came as a shock when I suddenly understood that early next morning we would arrive at Ichang. The nice safe bubble that I had been living in was about to break.

CHAPTER TWELVE
UP THE YANGTZE GORGES

I WAS looking forward to seeing Johnson Mead again and had been writing to him to let him know my movements, but he had not been able to send me an answer so I was afraid I might have trouble in finding him. As the boat came alongside it was a great relief to see a tall, foreign figure standing there, especially as the coolies on shore were already screaming and shouting for custom. When they realized that I was the person Johnson had come to meet they left me alone. As we walked through the crowded streets towards the mission house that he was sharing with the doctor and his wife, he told me that the next part of the trip up-river would not be nearly as comfortable as the piece I had just done; the river was still falling, and at each of the two stops on the way to Chungking we would have to change onto a smaller boat of lower draught, and the number of passengers would probably increase as the boats became smaller.

The few days in Ichang were a great help to me. At last I was among people who were not trying to put me off my trip but were out to make it a success. I ordered a Chinese dress. At first the idea was that I should have a long one, like the better-class Chinese, with a slit up to my knee. But that would mean wearing stockings and a suspender-belt, and besides, it would have been terribly cold. So we compromised on my corduroy trousers with a coat to the knee, which made me definitely middle class, for it was longer than the peasants' and shorter than the ladies'. Then I bought a Chinese bag with compartments for my money and my papers; it was made of blue cotton and had a couple of tapes which they tied round their waists underneath their clothes. The Chinese could wear these bags so they did not show, but whether I had more money or more papers or simply there was more of me, it stuck out most noticeably when I wore it.

Then there were the conversation cards so that I could explain such basic wants as: "That is too expensive," "Please bring some food," "Give me a ticket to ...," "Some boiling water, please." The cards were to be in red, the colour of happiness, and the phrases were to be written by the best calligrapher in Ichang.

We approached him most respectfully. It was like going to order a set of pictures from a world-famous artist. He was a fine-looking man in his late 30s, and he invited us into his house for some tea. There we began the formal conversation necessary as a preliminary to the purchase of works of art. Johnson gave me a very good build-up.

"This lady is a great admirer of the Chinese and although she has very little money she has come a long way to visit China and is travelling into the interior away from the big foreign cities so that she can meet them and try to feel at home among them."

Here there was an interruption while the artist bowed to me and I bowed and grinned back.

"As she has not been able to learn the language, we thought that a few cards with phrases written on them would make it easier. If they are written by a real artist, the people who read them will know that she appreciates their art."

This speech seemed to be going down very well, so I bowed and smiled again. But it was difficult for a foreigner to be charming to the Chinese, for they find most of us so ugly as to be almost painful. Fortunately, they quite like looking at freaks. I made rather a good freak with my fair hair, big bones and grey eyes, which Chinese only have when they are blind. Still, it does not give you much confidence when you are trying to persuade people to like you. He was a nice man and recognized that I was trying to do my best. He agreed to make the cards and have them done by the next day.

As we were walking back, we passed a building that looked like a temple but was painted white and pale blue and was so full of beds that it looked like a hospital. It was in fact both, as many of the temples were, having been converted into hospitals for the casualties from the war with the Japanese. This war was rather peculiar as it was not officially declared. The main fighting was not actually in China itself, where the warlords and Communists were keeping Chiang Kai-shek's troops busy, but in the Outer Territories round Inner Mongolia and Manchuria which the Japanese claimed did not belong to China anyway.

We went in to see the hospital. Most of the wards were filled with civilians from Ichang, but there was one huge ward that was absolutely packed with wounded soldiers. There must have been 50 of them lying there, all swathed in bandages. They had come in only the night before. I was tremendously interested and sympathetic.

"Was it a big battle?" I asked. "Where were they wounded?"

The young Chinese nurse answered me in English: "Last night in the theatre."

It was quite true. One company had gone in and sat themselves down in the front rows. When the other company arrived they could not see the stage well enough so they drew their guns and attacked in close order.

The hospital was far better than the ones I had seen in the south of Russia. It was cleaner, looked more efficient, and the patients were far gayer. Perhaps this was due only to the temperament of the Chinese, who never seem to give way to despair or let circumstances overwhelm them.

After only two days in Ichang I found that I had managed to get so much done that it looked as if I would be able to catch the next boat that came in. This time I was looking forward to it and was confidently equipped with an enamel basin and mug, my Chinese dress, and my new conversation cards.

When the boat came in, it turned out to be quite different from the first one. It was much smaller, with big, old-fashioned paddle-wheels, but the bird-cages were out over the stern as usual. It had no huge, barn-like sleeping quarters, though there were a few cabins, but I was a deck passenger and had to sleep on deck. My connection with the missionaries who, in a town like Ichang where there were no other foreigners, counted pretty high in the social scale, enabled me to claim a good piece of deck space with a bit of privacy; I also had some protection from the weather which, though sunny, was remarkably cold.

I said good-bye to Johnson and felt a little ashamed at being unable to hide my excitement at leaving; it seemed so ungrateful as it was all due to his help and advice that I was feeling so carefree.

There was a grinding noise from the engines, screams from the ship's siren — which were almost drowned by the crescendo of yells from the passengers and their friends — and then we were off. I hardly had time to arrange my deck space, or so it seemed, before we were entering the Yangtze Gorges. The boat, dwarfed by the high cliffs, groaned and shuddered her way against the tremendous current. I got a crick in my neck looking up at the heights, but I soon found that there were plenty of more exciting things to look at lower down. Along the cliff-face were the paths for the coolies who towed the junks up-river, and now, with so few steamers able to run, there were more junks than ever. Sometimes the paths ran fairly near the river and I could see the faces of the men as they pulled. Then, if the cliff close to the river became too vertical for even the Chinese to make a track across it, they would have to climb so high they looked like flies on a wall.

The junks coming down were the most exciting to watch. At least two men would be on the steering-oar, and sometimes they would have a struggle to avoid a bad whirlpool or a dangerous rock. For the junks it was more dangerous to come down-river than go up, but all the same their owners would load them with far more than they could safely carry, which made them even more difficult to steer.

At dinner-time I found that the food was just as good as on the previous boat, and by now I could hold my own with my chopsticks and was beginning to recognize some of the dishes.

In the afternoon one of the crew came and spoke to me. I could not understand what he said but he looked friendly, so when he signed to me to follow him, I did. He led me up to the bridge. A large man with a slightly Chinese face got up from a curious high stool and came and shook my hand.

"Captain Müller," he said and bowed. "I thought that, as you are a foreign lady, you would like to come and use the bridge which is more comfortable for you than the deck."

The bridge stretched right across the boat and was fairly high and glassed in. Now I could keep warm and see absolutely everything that went on. At first I thought that Captain Müller was anxious to practise his English, but after a while I realized that he was looking for someone who would take an interest in his piles.

Apart from the navigation, they were his main preoccupation. I was not spared one ghastly detail of his sufferings. The chair he sat on had been specially designed by himself, the seat being made with a hole in the middle like one of those rubber rings supplied to bedridden patients in hospitals.

In spite of the main topic of conversation, I enjoyed this part of the trip. Sometimes I was invited to use the special chair, and very comfortable it was, and sometimes he would tell me about his life. He never mentioned his mother and he implied that he was a full-blooded German, but he told me quite a lot about his Chinese wife. Theirs had been an old-fashioned Chinese marriage and they had not seen each other until after the wedding.

"I think that way is better," he said. "We both knew we would have to make the best of it, and we are very happy now. More people want divorce who married for love than who married for duty."

It was difficult to judge by his case, for he had always been working on the river steamers while his wife stayed at home with the family.

I was sorry when we reached the village where his steamer had to stop because the river became too shallow for her to go any higher. We were to transfer to another boat of shallower draught, but she had not arrived yet and no one seemed certain when she was expected. As she would be coming downstream I thought it would be a wonderful opportunity for me to nip up and see the cliff-tracks that for centuries had been used by the coolies towing junks up to Chungking. It was an almost vertical climb and the track was horrifyingly narrow. I suppose that if there were several men pulling on the same rope it would hold one man if he slipped and fell. When I had climbed high up the cliff I could not bear to go back down again and determined to climb right to the top. I had had little exercise in the last few weeks, so I was sweating and gasping by the time I got there and was only too glad to find a rough track which sloped instead of dropping almost vertically back in the direction that I wanted to go.

Out of the shelter of the gorges it was cold but sunny and there were young shoots of green pushing up through the brown earth. I could not see one human being. To be absolutely alone in the fresh air was bliss. Walking easily in my cotton shoes along the dusty track, losing the height I had sweated to gain, I rounded a bend that brought me out once more over the river. There were a few people about. Their houses had been hollowed out of the cliff with just a façade of mud in front, pierced by two windows and a door. The inhabitants were as surprised to see me as I was them, but they recovered before I did and soon they were pressed around me, fingering my clothes and, with tentative pushes, trying to find out my sex. One very jolly woman waved the rest away and, seizing my arm, tried to get me onto the path leading to her house. As it was not the way I wanted to go I stood firm. She dropped my arm and calling loudly "Wait! Wait!" ran into the house and came back in an instant with a handful of freshly roasted popcorn. She held it out to me and as I greedily reached for it she retreated a step, and in no time with this donkey-and-carrot method she had lured me inside her house.

The whole family were sitting down to their evening meal. There were at least ten of them of various ages. They all stood up and urged me with unmistakable gestures to join them. After my hors d'oeuvres of popcorn I was ravenous and sat down on a three-legged stool in front of a big bowl of noodles and pork. My first bite was a disaster. It was like a mouthful of molten lead. My mouth hung open, my nose streamed, tears fell from my eyes, and I have no doubt that I moaned. The young man sitting next to me acted promptly: seizing a bit of it from his bowl with his chopsticks, he sucked the sauce off it and then popped it into my still-open mouth, making signs to me to suck. Almost at once I felt relief, and while I was wondering how I could politely refuse further hospitality, the sound of a boat's siren came up from the river.

I shot to my feet and out of the house, hoping that I was saying, "Thank you, but I must catch my boat."

They all laughed and waved, so it seemed they understood. I rushed down the hill as fast as I could go. Now that I was on the cliff-path I could see the boats below me and it looked as if the boat I wanted to catch was ready to leave. The one I had come up in was on her way down-river. I was at my last gasp when I arrived at the gang-plank. Some people whom I recognized as fellow-passengers off the other boat came running down; they seized me by each arm and rushed me up to the deck. There they took me to where they had already put my luggage. They bowed and made little deprecating gestures with their hands when I tried to thank them; then they slipped quickly away into the crowd.

I sat down and looked round. The deck was packed, and I noticed that there were quite a few soldiers among the crowd. My helpers had put my bags down on the deck beside one of the wooden boxes that were labelled "Life-Jackets", but there was scarcely room to sit, let alone lie down for the night. I climbed on the box and tried it out as a possible bed. It was better than the deck-space and fairly wide, but I had to lie curled up like an embryo or let my legs dangle over the edge. The evening meal was disappointing, but this was obviously because the boat was so crowded, its kitchen being designed for only a third of the number of passengers that were now aboard.

I dropped off quickly to sleep after all the exercise, but at first I seemed to wake up every five minutes to pull up my legs which kept slipping over the edge of my box. It was broad daylight when I woke up after an unexpectedly long sleep, and I realized that one of the passengers must have taken pity on me for there was a pile of boxes and bundles pushed up against the life-jacket box, level with the top and supporting my feet. In no other country, I felt, would the Good Samaritan have been content to remain anonymous.

It turned out to be an exciting day. By ten o'clock the poor old boat was finding it almost impossible to make headway against the current. Smoke was pouring out of the funnel, which was red-hot in places, and any small object that was not fastened down soon jiggled its way into the scuppers. Ahead, the river took a right-angled bend, so the tremendous cliffs on either side seemed to have shut us in. The water coming out of the shadow on the right was not visible until it reached a band of sunlight at the foot of the cliff ahead. It looked as if it had sprung sparkling into the canyon and was rushing down towards us. The river was so low that we could see quite clearly that there was a definite drop of about a foot in the water-level. There was no way around, and the boat could make no headway. We were stationary at the foot of this little waterfall and quite incapable of putting on any more speed.

The crew gathered together to decide how to deal with the crisis, for the ship seemed to be run on completely democratic lines. The chief engineer came up from below with some grease-covered figures, the deck crew gathered round, and they all went to the bow, where the captain was standing. There was a big winch wound with wire cable. It looked rather forlorn and rusty but the engineer gave it a couple of heavy blows with a large spanner and said something that made the rest all laugh. Then four sailors lowered a dinghy and filled it with a huge straw rope. They fastened one end to the cable on the winch and then rowed off as fast as they could for the shore, with two rowing and two bailing.

The engineer's assistants got to work on the winch, and by the time the men with the rope reached the shore, the drum was turning slowly.

We could easily see the four figures on shore struggling to drag the grass rope to a pinnacle of rock. When at last they got there they started to haul out the rusty wire cable, while on our boat the engineers struggled over the engine for the winch.

Earlier on in my journey I might have felt a bit nervous as I watched the rusty wire with its broken strands go jerkily out over the bow, to be pulled laboriously ashore where it would be made fast to the pinnacle of rock and then used to pull us up the little waterfall. By now I had as much confidence in the Chinese as they had in themselves, perhaps more, for they were Buddhists and believed in predestination; they did not think the condition of the cable was very important. The groanings of the winch were dreadful to hear when it finally took the load and slowly inched the boat up the fall. I really thought the teeth would be shaken out of my head by the vibrations of the main engine and the winch. The passengers enjoyed the whole performance, giving advice, applauding the rowers, and laughing at the jerking winch.

Near me was a well-dressed but rather untidy young woman whom I had seen in company with a magnificent Chinese officer. She smiled at me and, when the excitement was over, we moved to the stern, where it was a little quieter. Conversation was very difficult, for my Chinese never had much chance of improving: with each day's journey the local dialect changed and I had to learn another pronunciation for the same words. She took me to her cabin, as she was travelling first class, and there she unpacked her trunks and showed me the most amazing collection of beautiful clothes, all in Chinese style, but made from really valuable brocades and lined with mink, snow-leopard, and other expensive-looking furs. I was bursting with curiosity: these were the clothes of an aristocrat and, though attractive enough to look at, she was clearly of peasant stock. Visions of battles and plunder passed through my head, but perhaps there was a more humdrum explanation. She also had a servant and, while we were admiring and trying on the clothes, he served us with the best tea I have ever had. It was a lovely golden colour and as stimulating as alcohol. It was a great piece of luck, as she took a fancy to me, and over the next couple of days I was frequently invited to her cabin for tea and snacks. This made a lot of difference, for the ship's meals became worse and worse.

When we reached Wanhsien the troops all left, and so did my friend and her colonel. I was expecting to change boats again here but found that the one I was on was going on to Chungking. In the interval after the old passengers left and before the new ones came aboard I was able to stake a claim to a nice, secluded piece of deck for my bed. To my horror I saw some Europeans coming up the gang-plank. I had not been on my own long enough to be lonely for my own kind. On the contrary, it gave me a great lift to be the only foreigner among the Chinese, and there was a good reason for this feeling, for as soon as they saw that a foreigner was not alone they ceased to help.

The new arrivals turned out to be missionaries going up to Chungking. They were very friendly but they could not understand why I was travelling at all in this part of China. The people did not seem to interest them except as possible converts and they had been so many times up and down the Yangtze that they were impervious to the scenery and felt very put out that the river was too low for the foreign boats to run. They were particularly distressed by the bird-cages over the stern, for the other boats had normal ships' lavatories.

As we came nearer to Chungking the gorges were less impressive and the country less desolate. Chungking itself was wonderful, with the flight of steps leading up from the river, and the people washing, and the grunting chant of the constant procession of heavily laden water-coolies.

I followed the missionaries to the mission hostel. Chungking was a jumping-off place for many mission stations; the gorges were a kind of bottle-neck up which the missionaries had to travel in order to reach the interior, but once past them they could spread out north, south and west. Naturally, the missionaries stationed in Chungking itself could not possibly cope with this constant stream of people by inviting them into their homes as they did in the more isolated places. So the various missions had clubbed together and taken a house that was run as an interdenominational hostel and at very reasonable rates.

It was not far from the top of the steps, so we did not need rickshaws. I hated to use them but at the same time felt that I ought to do so, for the coolies needed every passenger they could get; they were such pathetic figures, with the most terrible varicose veins. They were so small and thin that I was afraid one day the same thing might happen to me that I saw happen that day in Chungking to a large, fat merchant who had come off our boat with several bundles. He got into a rickshaw and leant forward to tell the coolie where to go. Then the coolie picked up the shafts just at the same moment as the passenger leant back. A second later, rickshaw and merchant were flat on their backs while the coolie hung in the shafts, pawing the air with his feet as he tried to reach the ground.

Living in the mission house was not very amusing. There were too many foreigners about for the Chinese to take any interest in me. The main excitement was the fire that took place every night in the area where the refugees were squatting. There were so many fires and the refugees were so pathetic that I quite dreaded the evenings. I wanted to get away from Chungking as quickly as possible.

CHAPTER THIRTEEN
THE BURSTING BUS

I NOW had to arrange to go the next stage of the journey by bus. In this part of China there were no railways but only roads and rivers. The rivers had been the highways for thousands of years and the roads had been narrow as befitted coolie and wheelbarrow traffic. But now since Chiang Kai-shek had come into power, the government had been making roads wide enough to take buses and lorries, and the Chinese had taken eagerly to these new forms of transport. The buses started from a point on the outside of the old city, for the streets inside the city were far too narrow for them. Two days after I arrived I was able to book a place in a bus leaving next morning for Chengtu, about three days' journey away.

A bus, unlike a train, when full to bursting, bursts; and in China this does not take very long to happen. The one I caught from Chungking had only recently given way; the original paint was still in fairly good condition and you could clearly see the strips of unpainted metal where the seams had burst. I think that on the whole the owners are quite glad when this happens for it means that there is room for more people. The glass in the windows had now been replaced by iron bars and the emergency exit was firmly fixed with iron staples. The roof, roughly put back where it originally belonged, was lashed on with wire. I wish I had witnessed the wonderful moment of bursting when the people crammed through the doors so hard that they forced the early settlers to rise slowly out of the top.

The fact that I was a large, foreign female, from whom absolutely nothing was expected in the way of manners, helped me to force my way into the bus where, with great pride in my planning, I managed to grab a seat by the window. I got my bundles under my feet and more or less rested my head on my knees, then I relaxed and began to enjoy myself.

The shouting and yelling of the passengers was reaching the usual climax before the bus started: fists were shaken, teeth bared, a few blows exchanged. The driver's accomplice forced himself in, locked what was left of the door with a padlock and chain, threw a lighted cigarette butt on top of the petrol tank near the filler-cap, and with a roar we were off.

The street we went through was the scene of the previous night's fire; families were salvaging what they could of their own — and possibly their neighbour's — goods, and resurrecting kerosene tins and anything else that had not burnt. It all looked very normal and, as a piece of the town burnt down every night, no doubt it was.

Then suddenly we were in the country; it was lovely, neat and specklessly tidy. Everything had a purpose and the people working had that pride and dignity which there seemed to be no time for in the towns.

I was happily sniffing in the scented air when I was butted in the side by a frantic head making its way to be sick through the window, but the bars were set too close and there was only me. Unfortunately, Chinese buses did not seem to break down nearly as often as the Persian ones, and for at least another hour desperate heads of various sexes tried unavailingly to pass the bars. By the time we stopped I had firmly decided that however beautiful the scenery I was going to stick to a middle seat from now on.

Chiang Kai-shek's government had started a movement for cleaner inns, and the buses nearly always stopped at inns which showed signs of that good work. They were usually temples painted blue and white, and on the whole I liked them. The sheets on the wooden beds were changed about twice a week and looked quite clean, and the people had a pleasant air of wanting to oblige. The first one we stopped at was for a lunch halt, and here I found the best way of paying. I would point to what I wanted and, when it arrived and I had eaten it, I would hand my purse over to one of the other passengers and with graphic signs ask him to pay the bill for me. In this way I seemed to have the best of both worlds. The terrific *esprit de corps* which had already been generated on the bus made the passenger bargain furiously on my behalf, and the waiter poured his abuse not on me but on the holder of my purse.

When we all climbed back into the bus there was quite a different atmosphere. We, the original passengers, were friends now, loyal allies against anyone who should try to get in. It was safe to leave my luggage and my seat and wander round during the halts; I always found that someone was looking after them when I got back.

This sort of travel makes me terribly lavatory-conscious, and I was enchanted to see the arrangement made by farmers keen to attract valuable manure to their fields. Just off the roadside a nice little ditch would be dug with a few boards across and sometimes — a real coaxer — a little shed. Enough was left in the ditch to make clear what it was for so that, provided there were enough passers-by, the fields would be sure of their top-dressing. Certainly the fields looked well cared for. It was early spring up here and not yet too dusty; the whole landscape seemed so fresh and tender. But I always missed cattle in China; the country looked so different without them and it seemed so odd that all those millions could live and eat so well without milk, butter, cheese and beef. There were a few water-buffalo but otherwise there were no edible animals except pigs and dogs.

We stopped for the night at an old-fashioned inn, all dark wood and mysterious smells in corners. It was crammed with people and there was no hope of getting a bed, but my fellow-passengers found me a dark little nook to myself on the floor. After some women had gone all through my bundle and had tried on my clothes, I knew it would be safe for me to leave my belongings with them while I went to look for an eating place.

It was only a small town and there was not much choice. This did not matter very much, for all Chinese food is so good. I sat down and when the waiter came I held up my cards that said "Please bring me some food" and "I do not rejoice in soup" keeping handy the ones with "How much is this?" and "It is too expensive." I stuffed myself full and, when the hot water came round at the end of the meal, I made sure that none of my fellow-passengers were looking at me and then tried a good sloosh and spit with the hot water as the Chinese did. It was terribly hot and I nearly took the skin off the inside of my mouth, but it was a marvellous way of getting rid of the rice particles and great fun shooting them out on the floor. So, feeling very adaptable, I went off to try my first night on my own in a Chinese inn.

It was quite dark and a surly man gave me a very primitive little light — just a wick in a saucer of vegetable oil — but enough to show me my sleeping-bag. It all began to seem rather unsavoury and by now my courage was non-existent, so I shot straight into my bag, blew out the light and waited for sleep. I felt as if I were not sleeping a wink, but I suppose I must have dropped off quite quickly for I was suddenly woken by an awful stabbing pain in my right ear. With a loud yell I sat bolt upright and laid about me in the dark. There was confused shouting from the next-door room and a figure burst in with an electric torch which lit up in a ghastly fashion the flying forms of dozens of enormous rats. I put my hand up to my ear and it came away sticky with blood where one of them had bitten me. This was living like the Chinese with a vengeance.

The man with the torch shouted something and in no time the room was full of people all offering advice and beating the corners with sticks. Then a very distinguished figure appeared. He was one of the bus passengers but a most superior man. He wore Chinese robes and seemed to have an entourage of three or four people: one of them was obviously a servant, but the others were harder to place; they might have been members of his family or perhaps secretaries. As soon as he arrived silence fell and we all waited for him to speak. He said something to the innkeeper who ran off and came back with two much better lamps and a bowl of hot water and a cloth. Then, while I bathed my ear, he directed the innkeeper to put one of the lights at my head and the other at my feet and made me understand that the lights would keep the rats away.

Then he spoke quietly to the rest of the crowd and off they went just like lambs. He then came and looked at my ear, made a soothing noise, bowed his head graciously and left. This made an extraordinary impression on me and I felt that even the rats must be affected, so I lay down and in no time was asleep.

Next morning I was woken up by the great man's servant bringing me a bowl of soup with dumplings, and when I went out to the courtyard where the bus was waiting I found him standing with the two secretaries. I went across to try to thank him, but he merely inclined his head and motioned me to stand behind him.

When the bus driver opened the door we all went in first while the other passengers waited, and I was put in a seat behind this man who seemed to have made himself my protector. All the other passengers then crowded in and, behind his back, with nods and smiles, showed that they thought I had done pretty well for myself.

It was a lovely drive — so far away from anything foreign. I did not see a single Chinese in European dress and some of the towns we passed were almost completely surrounded by their ancient walls. The scenery was growing wilder and the weather colder. I enjoyed being part of an entourage and being ordered about by waves of the hand and nods of the head, for he never addressed a word to me.

That night we stopped at a country place, and he gave orders for a woman to show me around and I was put in a nice room by myself with lots of hot water to wash in. Then just as I was wondering about dinner, a secretary arrived, beckoning, and I followed him to a separate room where the master was already seated at a table covered with little dishes. He made a sign for me to sit down, and we had some sunflower seeds and various other things that were all delicious but quite unidentifiable. Then came the main meal and warm wine in little cups. There was a proper way to drink it — not as I did, just gulping it down when I felt like it. That, I soon realized, was very poor manners indeed, so I waited till someone lifted their cup first, looked at me and gave a little bow, then I took my cup, made a little bow and drank it down.

Everything seemed to be going well, and I managed to say "Good" in Chinese several times, then the last serving of rice came round, and the final tea. I felt that the company was too exalted for me to do my rinse-and-spit, so I contented myself with laying my chopsticks across the top of my bowl and tipping it towards the rest of the company with a graceful bow as I had seen all the others do. But to my disappointment, no sooner had I put the bowl back on the table than an unmistakable gesture from my host made it only too clear that I was expected to leave. It was a blow, for I had been having such fun. I hoped that it was merely because I was the only woman that I was being made to leave.

Next day was the last on the bus. I was still in the entourage, well looked after and beginning to be well organized, although I was only an appendage and communicated only by signs.

We arrived at Chengtu at about three in the afternoon. The Quaker college where I was going was some little way out of the city itself, and so I had to hire a coolie to take my bundle and show me the way. This was also arranged for me, and when I bowed good-bye and tried to express my thanks, the great man replied with only the faintest of smiles and a dismissing wave of the hand.

By now we seemed to be back in winter. There was snow on the ground and an icy wind blew straight from Tibet. The coolie took a short cut over the frozen fields and my feet felt the cold in my cotton-soled shoes. I walked along with my head bowed to the wind, just keeping the coolie's legs in view, until at last I happened to look up to see if I was missing anything, and there was a foreigner coming towards me. I reacted just as a Chinese must do at his first sight of one. I was terrified of the tall, angular figure with enormous arms and legs, scarlet face and big hooked nose under a black wideawake hat, black mittens with huge red fingers poking through, and, most striking of all, straw sandals with red, gnarled toes sticking out of them. I stopped with a gasp, unable to believe that we could look so alien to people of another race, and I felt a surge of gratitude to the Chinese who, in spite of my grotesque appearance, had been so kind to me.

The figure advanced towards me and shook me firmly by the hand.

"You must be the lady we are expecting," he said, "and I am very glad to see that you believe in Chinese footwear. I suffered all my life from chilblains until I took to wearing these sandals."

CHAPTER FOURTEEN
THE GOD OF THE MIN RIVER

CHENGTU was an attractive old town which still stood within its own walls. Here there were no longer the refugees who were crammed into Chungking, though many families had their houses filled to bursting with relatives who had fled from the Japanese. As yet they were only the better-off people, so there were none of the piteous poor with all their goods on one wheelbarrow and nowhere to shelter for the night.

The Quaker college was the only sign of modernity in Chengtu, and in any case it was outside the town walls and away from all the hubbub. Even the Chinese students in this university quarter seemed to have imbibed the quiet, reposeful air of the Quakers. I enjoyed the complete change of atmosphere; indeed, I think that is one of the things that makes travelling such fun. I love Chinese food, so gastronomically I enjoyed being with the Chinese best, but a room to myself, with a window that let in nothing but fresh air and the scent of earth and trees, was a luxury that I could not tire of.

The college had its own printing press upon which they had produced a very attractive book about Mount Omei and its famous temples. I had heard of this book as far away as Changsha and had been looking forward to buying a copy, particularly as I was now determined to climb Mount Omei myself. It was only a couple of days' journey in the bus to Kiating, where I would have to start walking, and at Kiating there was a mission where I would be able to get help in hiring coolies. The book gave a full description of the path up the mountain and all the temples on the way, and it was illustrated with lovely Chinese engravings of the places on the route. It was written in Chinese and English, and printed on fine Chinese paper with the texts on facing pages. I had never seen a book I liked so much, and I had certainly never owned one; the characters and pictures were works of art in themselves and it was surprisingly cheap too.

I went down to the walled city and bought a piece of oiled paper to wrap the book up in. Chengtu was the first town that I had seen which seemed to be adjusting itself gradually to the strain of the present. Szechuan was a fertile province and had lived a very independent life. As it was self-supporting and almost out of reach of the Nanking government, it had been run by warlords. Now with the government in Chungking, it was becoming more orderly. After Chungking, Chengtu seemed to have much less crowded streets, but the greatest relief to me was that there were none of the pathetic structures made from old tins, blankets and cardboard, and filled with families on the verge of starvation.

There was room to wander about and look at the different streets, each one devoted to a different trade: silversmiths, coppersmiths and, most glamorous of all, the embroiderers. Even in their embroiderers the Chinese were different from the rest of the world, for these artists were all men. They sat on heated seats, raised up above the crowd, and worked at an interesting job where they could talk to passers-by and see a lot of what went on in their city.

I felt quite a dramatic figure as I said good-bye at the crack of dawn to the friends I had been staying with and followed my coolie to the outskirts of the town to catch the bus, for I was going to travel through an area where some Europeans had been killed and others had disappeared. I had heard plenty of stories about buses being held up and Europeans being taken for ransom. In general it seemed that the Americans and English were taken for ransom and so usually stayed alive, while people of other nations were usually killed. One unfortunate Turk, who was a bicycle salesman, had been killed only two weeks before while travelling on the same road to Kiating. Whether the Chinese had heard the same stories and thought that I would be a dangerous fellow-passenger, I do not know, but certainly the bus was nothing like so crowded as it had been on my earlier bus journey.

The bus itself was much worse; no two bits seemed to be of the same vintage, and even the wheels looked uneven. I carefully took

my seat plumb in the middle, put the rucksack on the roof and my
baifu and food packet in with me. This time there was none of the
hysterical excitement there had been when we set off from
Chungking. Perhaps it had been due to the strain of the war. At all
events I never felt, as we pushed our way into the bus, that this
time my neighbours would have been delighted by my sudden
death. Even the shouts seemed to be friendly farewells rather than
gruesome threats.

The day was bright and sunny. The road must have been a river
in the flood season and I liked the magnificently powerful and
almost serpentine way the bus tackled the boulders. We were travelling south, and the foothills with the eternal snows behind them
were on the right — once or twice I could see them — and I
thought that the country people seemed to have a more virile and
independent look. The country itself on the right side looked less
subservient to man, and that tonic in the air, which I always feel
near mountains, made the hours fly by. There were a few of the
usual breakdowns, but I did not realize that anything was out of
the ordinary till the bus took a sharp turn to the left on what was
obviously a side road. With the aid of one of my conversation
cards and the name of the town where we were supposed to be
spending the night, I found out that owing to some engine
trouble, we were going to another place quite off the beaten track.
The minute we passed through the old walled town gate I could
see from the behaviour of the people that a bus was a rarity. They
pressed so closely round that at last it came to a complete stand-
still. The driver told us to get out. When I appeared, there was a
gasp of either horror or alarm, and the crowd pressed so tightly
round me that I was cut off from the bus.

These people were taller than the coastal Chinese, though most
of them were shorter than I, and as they pushed nearer it always
seemed to be the ones with running sores and unblown noses
whose faces brushed against my shoulders. By this time I could no
longer move my arms, and nasty prickles of panic began to upset
my thoughts. The crowd did not make much noise but only
murmured to each other and there was not a smile on any face. A
kind of hostility seemed to be in the air and the murmuring turned
into a menacing sort of hum, broken suddenly by a voice from the
outside of the scrum which seemed to be asking a question. The
answer given by those nearest me came as an appalling shock:

"Japanese!" they shouted back.

For a second I could not really believe that they had taken me for a Japanese, but it was imperative that they should not think so for long. Forcing my lips into a smile, my brain working overtime in the effort to remember some Chinese words, I managed to get out what I hoped was: "Me Englishwoman, Japanese bad."

The response was immediate; the ones near enough to have heard my words doubled up with laughter, which in no time spread through the crowd, and soon they were seizing my hands and shaking them, hitting me on the back so that I seemed to be in fresh danger from their friendliness.

Suddenly a loud, female voice gained ascendance over the rest of the babble and laughter, and the crowd let go of me and made a passage for a hefty youngish woman with a tremendously broad pockmarked face and an air of competent authority. She took my hand in hers and, forcing a path through the crowd, took me to a door in the wall that lined one side of the street. I had to stoop to go through, and as soon as we were inside she shut and bolted it with a bolt that would not have looked out-of-place in Dover Castle but seemed quite necessary under the circumstances, as the crowd outside set about banging and pushing at it as hard as they could.

At first I could not see very well for, after the sunlight, it seemed dark as a cave, and I was quite content to hold onto her hand as she led me through a few small rooms and across a courtyard to another room with a half-door. Inside was a bed and a cotton rug on the mud floor. We sat down together on the bed and she gave me a tremendous lecture. I am not sure what it was about but I could understand that she was saying that she had behaved splendidly. I entirely agreed with her and think that I managed to put in my words of thanks at just the right moments. A little maid brought in tea; it was delicious, paler than any I had had so far, and must have been of excellent quality for after four cups I felt as if I had had a bottle of champagne.

In most countries, no matter how little I understand of the language, I occasionally meet a person who, by staring me in the eye and talking slowly and impressively, can make me understand at least half of what they are saying, and here in my first hour of panic I had met one of them.

We chattered away, exchanging information about our ages, families, clothes and food. She sent the little maid off for my luggage, and when it arrived she had a blissful time unpacking it and trying on the clothes and tasting the Horlicks tablets.

All this time the crowd had stayed outside, giving a push to the door now and then, with a few bangs and an occasional shout. Now they became more persistent and started a steady rat-tat-tat. Pressing another cup of the exhilarating tea into my hand, she got up and left me, and I heard her parleying with the crowd through the locked door. It was quite effective, and by the time she came back they had stopped making a noise.

She was followed by a very superior-looking man who bowed and sat down and then started to question us. Again I noticed the queer way in which she could make me understand the questions he asked, merely by repeating them. The conversation cards were produced and greatly admired, and so were my camera and alarm clock. Then, after a cup of tea, he bowed himself away. During the next hour a few other chosen visitors came and went. The women were all shown my clothes, which seemed a shame for I had nothing nice with me and they must have had a poor idea of foreign clothes. The men were shown the camera and alarm clock and were obviously more impressed.

We then sat down to a delicious meal, with rice instead of noodles and less highly spiced than I had been having recently, so she must have been fairly well off. Then she told me to tidy up and, when I had done so, she took my hand again and led me into the street. The crowds of people were still there, but by shouting at them and hitting them she kept them at a comfortable distance. We walked through the narrow-walled street on a dirt track which led into a square, paved with big flagstones. There we sat down on a stone bench and held a kind of court. The people all filed by and had a good look, while special friends were treated to a little dissertation on my most striking features: my enormous feet and hands — as they seemed to the Chinese — my blind man's eyes and extraordinary fair hair. I had little experience of trying to charm people by being a freak and I was not at all sure what I was supposed to do. Some mothers brought their babies and made them touch me with their tiny hands, but I was rather dashed to see that it was only the boys who touched me; I was much too ugly for them to take any risks with the girls. Perhaps they were hoping that the boys would grow to a tremendous size by virtue of this very brief contact. The whole town must have been there, and I was beginning to wilt when my guardian angel at last gave the sign that we could go home.

It was dark inside the house and the little maid came running to light the lamps; lovely, earthenware sauceboat-shaped ones filled with vegetable oil, a cotton wick hanging over the spout. The light was romantic and very poor, but in my bedroom there was an ordinary European paraffin lamp.

My hostess, determined to know the very last detail about me, helped me undress and supervised my washing and only left when I was tucked up in between a pair of hand-embroidered sheets with my head stuck up on an iron-hard pillow embroidered in English with "Sweet Dreams" in purple and gold across the corner.

Next morning I left early after a good hot bowl of noodles and some gorgeous little pastries. It was quite a different crowd who took me to the bus, and I could hardly believe that these happy, friendly, joking people were the same ones who had so silently and remorselessly nearly frightened me to death the day before.

It was with genuine gratitude and emotion that I said good-bye to the strange woman who had looked after me so well. Why had she done it? I could not tell from her expression whether she was glad or sorry to see me go, but I hoped that if I was really the first foreigner she had seen, I had made her realize that we were well-meaning, if a bit dim-witted.

All day the bus crawled and bounded along the worst road I had met so far, but in spite of the mountains always in view I was so tired after a day of being a freak that I dozed much of the time. In the evening we stopped in a town that was quite accustomed to foreigners.

I told a coolie in my best Chinese (for the conversation cards were useless for the illiterate and I never met a coolie who could read) to take me to a hotel. He took me instead to the Catholic mission. A delightful French father met me and we had a pot of tea together. I told him how frightened I had been the night before.

"You were right to be frightened, without the language," he said, and a look of pain came into his eyes. "In the anti-foreign riots even though we spoke Chinese and were among people who knew us, the other brother in my mission was killed and I only just escaped."

His sad look stopped me from asking questions.

"There is a lady missionary," he went on, "Miss Jackson from the China Inland Mission here; she would be so pleased to see one of her own sex."

This seemed to be a tactful hint that I should move on, so off I went. The father was right about Miss Jackson being pleased to see me, so perhaps it was not only that he wanted to get rid of me. She was a tall, good-looking woman, dressed in Chinese dress, which lends so much dignity even to Europeans.

"Oh, come in," she said at once. "How lovely to see you! Come in, come in!"

She seized me by the arm, snatched the luggage from the coolie, put it down, told him to pick it up again, addressed him in English and me in Chinese, and gave a thorough performance of being deliriously pleased to see me. It was touching, as I am sure she was normally a very self-possessed woman.

Her little room was charming; she probably had no more than the other China Inland missionaries, who were the lowest paid of all the missions, but she had shown such good taste in furnishing it that I had not seen such an attractive room since I left Chungking. I was delighted and surprised.

She had a tiny, four-week-old baby that had been left on her doorstep a fortnight before. She picked her up for me to see.

"I do so love having her," she exclaimed. "Already I cannot think of life without her."

I was not such an optimist, and I could only think of the endless trouble she had let herself in for. As soon as the news got around, any other Chinese mother faced, as they too often were, with the choice of killing their daughters or leaving them on her doorstep, would obviously dump them on Miss Jackson.

During our meal a plump young Chinese arrived to feed the baby; she had one of her own but with plenty of milk she could easily manage another. She was very pleased with the arrangement, for she was given a daily ration of food; though, to make sure she did not give it to her husband or other children, she had to eat it on the premises. In the flickering lamplight the European woman knelt down by the cot and lovingly picked up the little Chinese baby, dressed in European baby clothes, then passed her to the young Chinese who took her and fed her with the air of one having to do her duty. There was something sad about it all, and

142

to me it somehow symbolized the kind-hearted bungling — with disastrous results — of so many Occidentals in the Orient.

Both meals being over, Miss Jackson sat playing with the baby and talking of her plans for the mission.

"I dream of the day when all the Chinese will be able to read," she said, "so that they can read the Bible for themselves. Then they will all become sincere Christians."

"Don't you think," I suggested nervously, "that perhaps they may prefer to read comics and detective stories, like so many people in the West?"

"Oh, no!" she exclaimed. "You don't really think that? That would be terrible."

I could see from her expression of horror that she had never even thought of such a thing. These missionaries were inspired by a tremendous dream; they were cut off from their own country and very often from their own race, so perhaps it was small wonder that their ideas were so divorced from reality. She must have known that in her own country there were very few people who read nothing but the Bible. Yet it came as a shock to her that the same thing might be true of the Chinese.

"Where were you during the anti-foreign riots?" I asked, to change the subject.

"In Ninghsien," she replied. "The people had been restless for some time and were beginning to be rude to me in the streets, but I was hoping that it would pass over as it so often had before."

She kissed the baby and carefully laid her back in the cradle. Then, standing with her head bent so that in the lamplight I could not see her face, she went on, "A message came from the pastor to say that I must leave my village as the rioters were expected to come through it. I thought I would have a day at least to pack, but one of the Christians came running to say that they were in sight of the village."

She was quiet a minute, then she went on. "There was so much to do, I did not know where to start. I would never have been able to get away, but the Lord came and helped me pack."

The next day's journey was not very long and we reached Kiating by three in the afternoon. Most of the journey I spent speculating on what Mr. Jones, the missionary at Kiating, would be like. Ever since I had reached Ichang I had been hearing about him from both missionaries and laymen. He had been in the

Boxer Rebellion and had escaped disguised as a Chinese. He had been on his own in China for so long that he almost began to think like a Chinese and so he had lost his original urge to make converts. And now he had become an almost legendary figure to the Chinese, who called him "The God of the Min River".

The mission house was very attractively placed on a hillside, with a garden full of flowers, and, as I plodded up, a dapper, white-haired figure came trotting down to meet me. I knew that Mr. Jones was being forced to retire because he was over 60 but he had certainly gone Chinese enough to have no wrinkles. With a hat on he might have been 30.

"So nice to see you," he said. "Your room is all ready. How was the journey?"

We walked on, and he went on talking: "My relief has come and things are in a bit of a muddle as I do not leave for another week. They are a young couple; Cram is the name."

It was pretty evident from the way he said "Cram" that there was friction in the house. I was babbling away about how kind they all were to put me up, especially when they were so busy, when he cut me short.

"Do you want any mending done?" he asked suddenly.

"Well, you see, I usually do my own."

"Of course, how silly of me, but is there anything else, like washing, you would like to have done?"

"I'm sure I could find something," I said.

He looked relieved and moved closer to say, with a faintly conspiratorial air: "There is a woman I have been helping by giving her my mending to do. She has four children and her husband is a rickshaw-man and does not earn enough for the family. I would like her to earn as much as possible while I am here, for I'm sure the Crams won't employ her after I leave."

"Why?"

He lowered his voice and came a little nearer. "When they run out of money, she works as a prostitute," he said.

He was certainly different from any of the other missionaries I had met. He was obviously very unhappy; it was bad enough to be leaving but he was driven nearly mad by the Crams who were taking over from him.

They were a very earnest young pair who had just arrived in China after two years among the North American Indians. It

144

would have been hard to find two people more different from Mr. Jones. They were full of faith and the conviction that unless the Chinese listened to them and became Christians at once they would all be consigned to hell-fire for evermore. This naturally made them feel they were doing the Chinese a good turn by coming over to save their souls and so they saw no reason to try to understand Chinese customs or to take any other interest in them.

Mr. Jones had built the mission house and, until the war with the Japanese, he had been entirely on his own, the only foreigner for miles around. He spoke Chinese fluently and loved the food; he was especially partial to the custom of settling all business arrangements in a tea-shop after many complicated and long-drawn-out preliminaries. He was not particularly interested in conversions; his object was to live as a true Christian and hope that his example would make the Chinese think that Christianity must be a religion worth joining. Unfortunately, the mission was run on funds contributed by Baptists in Canada who wanted to be sure they were getting plenty of baptisms for their money, and poor Mr. Jones had very few converts to baptize.

As soon as Mr. Jones heard I was interested in going up Mount Omei, he whisked me out into the town to arrange the permissions I should need. I could see that he was jumping at any excuse to escape from the mission house because missionaries from all the outlying districts were foregathering for a meeting, which was also a farewell to him, and this crush of Christians was beginning to get on his nerves.

He was leaving in a week's time and offered me a lift in his junk as far as the Yangtze, where we would meet the river steamer. The prospect of travelling all that way with such a knowledgeable and entertaining companion was too good to miss. But I was not sure if I would be back from Mount Omei in time.

"How many days do I need?" I asked.

"If you keep at it and the weather becomes no worse, you should be able to reach the top in three days. With a day at the top and two coming back, that makes six days in all. But you'll have to be ready to walk all day," he warned me.

"I'll certainly try to be back in time, and if I start tomorrow it'll give me an extra day."

Mr. Jones was delighted with this answer, and we went straight off to the army post, as I would have to have a guard. At first the colonel said six soldiers would be necessary. I was appalled. I knew that I was not expected to pay them, but all the same they would all have to be tipped. But when Mr. Jones told the colonel that I was going on foot with only one coolie, he rapidly revised his opinion of my importance and admitted that two soldiers would be enough.

This fixed, we went off to a tea-house to arrange about the coolie. We settled ourselves fairly near the road and Mr. Jones began to glow with pleasure at the prospect of a good gossip. Not a soul passed without speaking to him, and I could see how fond they were of him. Every now and then a dignified town councillor or a commercial magnate would come and join us for a cup of tea. However serious the conversation, it always ended in a good laugh. I was not at all sure how much of all this confabulation had anything to do with my coolie, but Mr. Jones was determined to make the most of his excuse to stay away from the mission as long as possible. It looked as if he would be there all day, so I said that I had better leave and go back to the mission to get my things ready for an early start.

"Tell the Crams that I am arranging your coolie and escort," he replied blithely. "I will be back later."

Mr. Jones's vitality was extraordinarily infectious and I was already benefiting from it. Two hours before, when I had first arrived, I was looking forward to having a wash and lying down on a clean bed and then spending a leisurely day in arranging my trip to Omei, yet here I was, fresh as a daisy and planning to start in the morning on a 20-mile walk — all because I had met "The God of the Min River".

I returned to find the Crams discussing an invitation to a Chinese dinner.

"We will have to go, dear," Mr. Cram was saying. "Perhaps you could cook me something plain before we go, and I could say I was not well and just eat rice."

"Well, yes, we could do that," she said, and then, turning to me, "Mr. Jones so loves these dinners we feel we must go while he is here, but of course when my husband is in charge we will refuse all except official dinners. The food is so disagreeable."

There was nothing I could say. I merely gave them Mr. Jones's message, told them that we had arranged for me to start in the morning, and excused myself so that I could go and pack.

146

Packing was simple. I just had to separate my things into three bundles: the *baifu* for the mountain, for it would go most easily on the coolie's carrying-pole; the rucksack for the stuff to be left at the mission; and a bundle of washing for the prostitute mother. Then I sat down on my bed and studied my book about Omei to try to decide which monasteries I would like to stay in, where to stop for lunch, and where to see special gods.

That evening at a dinner of boiled chicken, rice and steamed pudding, I asked Mr. Jones what would be the right amount for me to pay in the monasteries where I would be spending the nights.

"It's a very delicate question," he replied. "It all depends on your appearance, the amount of your luggage, the number of your servants, and the size of your escort. Perhaps it would be best if I gave you a letter to the chief abbots, saying that you have come all the way from England to see the Sacred Mountain, that you are most grateful for their hospitality, and that you are planning to pay 15 cents (about fourpence) a night for bed, breakfast and dinner. Then it will be easy for them to know what to give you in the way of accommodation and food."

After dinner I felt very tired, and I knew that my coolie was coming round at eight o'clock in the morning, but I noticed as I left the room on my way to bed that Mr. Jones was getting ready to go out to a tea-house again.

CHAPTER FIFTEEN
THE SACRED MOUNTAIN

NEXT morning, having slept like a log, I was full of excitement about my trip. The Crams and another missionary couple, who had just arrived by junk, at once began to damp my spirits.

"The coolie will go along all right if you keep your eye on him," said Mr. Cram. "They always try to take unnecessary rests too early in the day, and then you find it is too late to reach shelter for the night."

"Whatever you do, watch the soldiers," the other missionaries urged me. "They will steal anything they can lay hands on."

Mr. Cram handed me a note written in Chinese. "You will be spending the night in the mission room in Chungcha. If you give this note to the caretaker he will know that you have our permission to use the room. It is not very comfortable, as we only use it when we go there to give a service for the Christians living there."

A noise outside proclaimed the arrival of my coolie. He was not a very attractive-looking specimen: thin, with a long and rather pockmarked face. The Crams gave him my *baifu* and told him something, I am not sure what, but it was clear that he did not like anything about my baggage or their advice. Then suddenly Mr. Jones appeared, spoke a few words, introducing him to me as Li, and the coolie was transformed. He picked up my *baifu,* gave me a beaming smile and started down the path. I quickly shook hands with all the missionaries and followed him.

As we went through the town, I tried to start a conversation with Li. When I had said "Soldiers" to him twice in my best Chinese, he understood — at least he burst into a roar of laughter, said "Yes" and pointed ahead, which I took to mean that we were going to the barracks. There was streamlined efficiency at the barracks when we arrived; as soon as I showed myself, the sentry gave a shout and out came two soldiers with guns, bandoliers, umbrellas, and a small bundle of kit. They formed up ahead of me and the coolie, and away we went.

It was early spring and the ground was still bare, with a few small fields being ploughed, but the weather was cold and grey and a nasty little wind was blowing down from Tibet. The coolie and the soldiers laughed and chatted as they went along. Li had a very small bundle of his own on one end of his bamboo carrying-pole and my *baifu* was hardly larger at the other. He could not have carried so light a load since he was a child. The two soldiers were real country boys, with healthy red cheeks, and they were in a holiday mood enjoying everything. Every now and then they would take pity on my speechlessness and point out a stork or some other bird and repeat its name slowly and distinctly, and then they would double up with laughter at my efforts at Chinese pronunciation. I hoped to goodness they were taking me the right way. The path was a mere track — perhaps it was a short cut — but I was surprised to see no villages or houses or even people. Hitherto, the country had been so populous that I had become used to seeing people everywhere. Now there were not even any landmarks; it was all flat and there was no way of telling how we were progressing. We walked on and on, but the high land ahead did not seem to be getting much nearer.

A bird flew past the soldiers, and with shouts of laughter they unhitched their rifles and fired at it. They had not a hope of hitting it, but they obviously loved the noise. I was horrified because everyone had been telling me how desperately short of ammunition the Chinese Army was in its war against the Communists, the Japanese and the more combative warlords. As these soldiers were shooting partly to entertain me, I did not want to appear ungrateful, so I tried to divert their attention with a little Chinese conversation. This had the unfortunate effect of stopping them in their tracks. While we tried to understand each other, they crouched down in the field and started to draw houses and animals in the earth. Echoes of the breakfast conversation came back to me. "They will dawdle on the way," I had been told, so I said what I hoped was, "It is late, we must hurry," only to be greeted by loud laughter and cries of "Plenty of time!"

All the same, I was very keen to get on, for I did not want to miss the river trip with Mr. Jones. As it was so early in the year, the mountain would still be in snow and I might easily be held up for a day if we had a heavy fall of it. I sprang briskly to my feet and started off in a very determined manner. At once there were loud cries from all three of them, and Li came running after me, seized me by the shoulder and, turning me round in almost the opposite direction, gave me a little push along a path I had not noticed, before going back to pick up his bundles.

Gradually we began to meet a few people, and then in the distance I could make out some buildings with smoke coming from them. We all perked up at this sight, for it meant food. There were now a good many people on the road, and they started to question Li and the soldiers about me. Li burst into tremendous explanations and then suddenly drawing himself up on tiptoe he came out with a few words which I could recognize as the ones I most often used, and from the high, falsetto voice in which he said them I realized that he was giving an imitation of me. The audience was enraptured, but any feelings of indignation that I might have had were quickly soothed when they turned to me and, as far as I could understand, congratulated me on my few words.

The road-house was now in smelling distance, and we all pushed on as fast as we could. It was an eating-house of the simplest kind — just walls and a roof, with a floor of earth, and a few benches and tables. Li was sweet; he brought a chair and dusted it for me; he fetched a basin of hot water for me to wash my face and hands, and then he took my hand and led me to the kitchen to choose what I would like to eat.

The cooks in these inns were extraordinarily good, and never once did I have a bad meal. There are very few trees in China, except on sacred mountains, and the Chinese seldom use coal, for the cost of transporting it is far too high for the ordinary people. The commonest fuel consists of the dried stalks of rice, millet, soya bean and maize. Being so thin, these stalks burn very quickly, but the Chinese manage to cook on them by using very shallow, wide saucepans which are recessed into the mud stove with a shallow place beneath each one in which a fire-tender, usually a child, keeps the burning stalks evenly spread under the pans, adding a stalk here and another there at dizzying speed to keep up a bright, even flame.

Even in this eating-house at the back end of nowhere there was a wonderful array of food, but my choice was always hit and miss, for the dishes and the pronunciation of their names changed a little with each district, so I rarely got what I was expecting. I let Li choose for me — which he enjoyed doing — and then he chose his own. I paid for his food but not for the soldiers'.

During the meal I began worrying about the time again and so I bustled them off before they were ready to start and was very firm with them when they wanted to stop. The Crams had said we should reach the mission by five, and in this cold weather that seemed quite late enough. It was getting on for three now, and in front of us was the town in which I thought we should have had lunch. The road was now unmistakable, so I strode on ahead, deaf to the complaints from behind. I went in through the walled gateway and was about to march straight through when Li put on an extra burst of speed, overtook me and stopped me in front of a doorway.

"Mission," he said, pointing.

"Nonsense, it is only three o'clock," I replied haughtily.

He would not budge and shouted up at a window above the door. A man's head came out and said something in what, after a second or two, I recognized as English. We had indeed arrived and I had as usual spoilt the day by needless worrying.

It was a miserable little place and I would much sooner have gone to an inn, but I felt it would be rude to leave now, so in we went, up a dismal narrow staircase into a small room full of hymnals and lesson books. The caretaker, who seemed to be rather an unhappy man, brought down a camp-bed and fetched me some hot water, while Li and the soldiers buzzed round me, opening up the camp-bed and arranging my things. Then Li, after humming and hawing, asked for an advance of his wages, while the soldiers, giggling and pushing each other, tried to summon up the courage to ask for a little money too. My heart was softened to find they had brought me along so well and reliably and I gave them all some money, telling them to be sure to come really early in the morning as we would be getting to the harder part of the journey. They switched their smiles off and with solemn faces promised to be ready at seven-thirty.

151

I felt rather gloomy when they left; it was such a dreary little room. I went out and had a meal, but after the fun at lunch that too seemed dull, so back I went and lay down on the dismal little bed and read myself to sleep.

Next morning we were off bright and early. It was very cold, but not raining — indeed it looked as if the sun might even shine. The track was clear and uphill from the start, and all the time it got steeper. The soldiers, Li and I chattered and laughed. Whenever I tried any new Chinese words, Li would repeat them, standing on tiptoe and using his falsetto voice. The way became very steep and occasional patches of snow were lying here and there. We were coming into the trees now: plenty of firs and pines and a few rhododendrons. We passed little shrines and temples, and I enjoyed bringing out my book and comparing the illustrations with the real thing. The three men were fascinated when I showed it to them and explained about the English translation. It was lovely to watch their faces when they recognized a picture in the book, then they would insist that I showed them what was written about it in the book. They looked admiringly at the Chinese characters, not understanding a word, but that is the nice thing about Chinese writing: even if you cannot read it you can still enjoy looking at it. We stopped at a temple which had a famous statue of Buddha. They told me a legend about it and insisted that I should see whether it was in the book. Luckily it was, and the version there was pretty much the same as theirs. The path began to be really steep and one could only plug along with one's head well down, climbing through snow almost all the time. We met a few pilgrims coming down, but they were all chattering, while we were breathing heavily.

I had told Li and the soldiers where I wanted to spend the night and that I wanted to be back in Kiating in time to leave with Mr. Jones, and I had decided to trust them to get me there and not keep nagging them on the march, so when they suggested stopping for lunch at the next monastery, I agreed. We went into the big courtyard, where Li put down his bundles, struck a bell hanging there, and then waited. After a minute or two there was a shuffling noise and in came a little old man who looked as if he must be nearly a hundred. With his red monk's robes and his little wrinkled face he was like a garden ornament. We all bowed. I produced my book and showed him the illustration of his monastery and the gods we wanted to see. He clapped his hands with pleasure and told us to wait while he went off in the direction of what I hoped was the kitchen. Then he came back, beckoned to us to follow, and led us to the temple.

It was very like Tibet: there were the same chants and gloom and decorations you needed a torch to see, representations of the Wheel of Life and fierce, protecting gods. We bought incense sticks and we all chose different gods to make our offering to. I chose the one I liked the look of best, but the others chose theirs because they had some special request.

The little monk had left us in the temple and now he came back to say the meal was ready. It was served in an unheated room and we sat on low cushions that seemed to be stuffed with stones, while the food was put on the floor in front of us. It was not as good as it would have been in an eating-house, but as they were strict Buddhists it had to be entirely vegetarian and there were not even any eggs. I think it must have been a very poor monastery: up on the side of the mountain there was hardly any room for growing things and it would have been expensive to have them carried up from the plain. The pilgrims were only just starting to come again after the winter so the monks must have been short of cash. They had plenty of the gentle tolerance which Buddhism gives and which is different from the strained and harassed air of so many Christian missionaries who feel that they are not doing their best unless they are trying to convert people to their point of view or keep them up to the mark if they are already converted.

The cold prevented us from wasting any time over the meal, and I paid the monk rather more for it than I would have done in an eating-house, for there was no set price and the money was meant more as a contribution to the monastery.

In the afternoon the walk began to be a struggle, as most of the steps were covered with snow and where it had been kicked away it had turned into half-frozen slush. But our falls and slides and awkward grabs at trees kept Li and the soldiers in fits of laughter. When we met pilgrims coming down, we usually stopped to ask them about the route higher up. The increasing cold was rapidly cooling my ardour for sightseeing with the Mount Omei book and I was very glad when we reached the monastery where we were to stay the night. Li rang the bell, and when the monk came I solemnly handed him the letter that Mr. Jones had written. He took it carefully in both hands to show the respect that is due to the written word and trotted off to show it to the abbot himself.

Then I was ushered into a warm inner room and the abbot came to talk to me. He had a very patrician face and was taller than most of the Chinese. We sat down and I showed him my book, and with its help we got along quite easily for five minutes or so, and then he called a monk to show me to my sleeping-room. It was very small, with a wooden board on trestles and a good, warm, padded coverlet. Then the monk took me to a sort of hall where they brought me some food. The food here was excellent; it was obviously a much richer monastery than the previous one.

The light of the vegetable-oil lamps was far too weak for me to read by and I was glad when Li and the soldiers came back, having had their meal in less exclusive quarters. I had been given a brazier to keep me warm and we all huddled round it. I thought this would be a good opportunity to try out the Chinese pipe which I had bought but had not yet used. The stem was very long and the bowl was tiny; the tobacco was very beautiful and looked just like long, pale, golden hair. As I had never smoked one before, I gave it to Li to start. He took a couple of the long golden hairs, rolled them up into a ball, and put them in the bowl. Then he picked up a live coal from the fire and lit the pipe, but after two puffs the tobacco was finished, so he filled it up again and offered it to me with a bow. The taste was very good — slightly scented and mild. When I had finished I passed it to one of the soldiers, and we crouched round the brazier, passing the pipe from hand to hand.

If I had been able to take a really long journey with those three, I think I could have learnt a good deal of Chinese. We looked through the book to see if we could make the top next day, and they said that if we started early and the weather was all right we should be able to do it. So I set my alarm clock and we all went off to bed.

Next morning it was not yet light when I got up, but the monks were already up so there was hot water and a bowl of gruel to start us off. We went into the temple, now lined with monks sitting on the ground chanting, and there we lit our incense sticks for the God of Good Luck and went on our way.

It was terribly cold but lovely, with the frost glistening on every-thing. Li and the soldiers were wearing straw sandals over rags

154

wrapped round their feet. I was in the ordinary cloth shoes with a rag sole, and they did not grip on the frozen snow at all, so I was thankful to find that at the first monastery we passed there was a monk selling straw sandals. I bought three pairs, as they wear out very quickly, and put a pair on over my cloth shoes. It made an enormous difference, but they did not stop my feet from getting wet.

The mountain is only 200 feet below 10,000, and as we climbed we began to slow down as we felt the height. I determined to relax and leave the pace to Li; I would not rush him. So far he had not let me down; he had promised to do his best to get to the top and each day gave me more confidence in him. If it had not been for all that well-meant advice I would have trusted him from the start. We plodded on, with our heads as low as possible, looking surreptitiously at one another while each of us hoped that the other would stop but nobody wanted to be the first to do so. I was particularly determined not to be the first to stop, even though climbing with my head right down meant that I missed most of the view, but I kept a sharp eye on the time so as to be sure to stop at the first temple that looked like giving us a good lunch. This was an occasion when it paid to be a woman. If I had been a man, Li and the soldiers would not have hesitated to say they wanted a rest, but they were damned if they were going to say they were tired before a woman was.

At last the time for lunch came and with it, very fortunately, a temple. We bustled into the courtyard and had a grand welcome from the monks. After the cold wind outside, even the unheated courtyard felt warmer, and when they led us into a small inner room with a brazier, we reached the height of luxury. We had a splendid vegetarian meal; then the soldiers asked for a pipe, so we had a couple of pipes apiece and a quick trip to the temple to light our incense sticks before we went back to the climb.

I felt much better after lunch, especially as I had taken off my wet slippers and put on dry ones. The weather was holding, so the chances of making the top looked pretty good, and this time I did not hesitate to stop and admire the view. It was well worth it; we were now high enough to be above all the smaller hills, and the plain stretched enormous at our feet. And all the time the weather was improving and the sky showing more and more blue.

When we reached the top it was much bigger than I had expected, and there was a large and surprisingly luxurious monastery there. The monk in charge showed me to a lovely bedroom which was almost up to the Japanese standards. It was pleasantly painted and there were mats on the floor, screens on the wall and good coverlets on the bed, and a brazier was glowing already. It was all delightfully cosy. As I was going to spend two nights there, there would be plenty of time to see the temple and the scenery, so I just threw myself down on the bed and lay there until it was almost dark. Then a big gong boomed out and a monk came to tell me it was supper-time. I was the only person in the dining-hall. I supposed that all the men must be eating some-where else, for it seemed to be a very strict monastery; no hens were allowed, though they did have a few cocks. The food was very good and of surprising variety.

After dinner I went back to my room. There was a full moon and, as I wanted to see the view by its light, I set my alarm for 11 and went to sleep. At 11 I could hardly bear to get up, for the brazier had gone out and the room was bitterly cold.

Outside the room was a long passage, dimly lit by lamps consisting of a twist of cotton lying in an earthenware bowl of vegetable oil. The polished floor stretched ahead, and the rich colours on the walls, the golden, flickering lights, a faint scent of joss-sticks and the distant murmur of chanting all combined to make me feel as if I had been transported to another world.

Just on the outside of the building the monks had built eyries supported on little thin legs against the monastery wall, and I was trying to find one of them from which to see the view. A gentle pad-pad behind me made me turn, and there was one of the monks. He bowed as he passed me and then beckoned to me to follow. It was as well he came because the eyrie was farther away than I had thought and there were quite a few twists and turns before he opened a door onto one of the little verandahs.

The cold wind took my breath away. The moon was round and bright and some drifting clouds had given her a kind of halo. The pines had lost most of their snow in the wind, but on the ground it was thick and glistening. I held onto the wooden railing and leant over to look down the mountainside. It was an almost vertical drop down to the plain, and all up and down the mountainside was covered with brightly flickering lights like enormous fireflies. I stared at them, unbelieving, for I knew there was nothing there but trees — the slope was far too steep for houses — so this was just sheer magic.

But all the beauty could not keep me warm and a mental picture of my nice warm bed seemed even more attractive than the view, so I dashed back down the winding passages to my room.

Next day Li appeared before I had got up, so I asked him to bring me my breakfast in bed. Then, feeling in a princely mood, I gave him a little money and told him to come back early the next morning. After he had left I lay back among the pillows and started to map out a little tour of the summit with my Omei book.

Since leaving Hong Kong I had not been on my own or spent a night in such a comfortable bed in such an attractive room, and if it had not been for my nagging conscience I could have happily lain there all day and seen Omei only in the book.

Finally, at 11:30 I got up and went off to the temple to see the statues and paintings. Then I had a good lunch and went out into the crisp air to visit the look-out places and the sacred stones. There were myths about every inch of the summit, but I had eyes mostly for the tantalizing glimpses of the high Tibetan mountains that showed every now and then through the clouds.

I think that if enough people think about the same thing in the same place over many years, that place begins to take on a certain quality that one can feel quite clearly. Here, where all the pilgrims arriving at the summit must have felt happy at achieving their goal, the whole place seemed impregnated with happiness, but it is very difficult to know what comes from yourself and what from outside, so I may have been mistaken and all the monks who seemed so happy to me may really have been monuments of frustration.

Next day we made a hideous start. It was piercingly cold and a nasty sort of cross between snow and rain came driving down. We rushed, slipped and tumbled downhill and arrived at the dreary mission resthouse. In the dark Li and the soldiers took me there so firmly that I realized I would let them down if I insisted on going to the hotel. I stoically went out and ate a quick dinner and came back to find them still there in the mission resthouse. They had brought out the camp-bed and made it up; they had lit an oil-lamp, and I was so tired that it did not look too bad. They brought me some hot water and then I said good-night to them and they went outside.

As I washed and put on my pyjamas I heard whispers and giggles, but I pretended not to hear. It was not long before I was

157

in my sleeping-bag in bed. Immediately the door burst open and the three of them rushed in and surrounded the bed. Li and one soldier bent over me and, seizing me by the head and feet, rolled me over on my side, while the other soldier carefully placed both their rifles and all their ammunition in the bed. I was then rolled back on top of it and they smoothed the covers as well as they could. They patted me and the covers and made it quite clear that I was to be in charge of the arsenal for the night, and then they rushed out before I could protest. When they had gone I rather guiltily shifted the rifles from under me to under the bed and set the alarm so that they would not surprise me not doing my duty in the morning.

I was up in plenty of time, had closed up my bed and tidied the room before Li appeared, very apologetic and looking rather the worse for wear. The soldiers arrived soon afterwards and took up their rifles and thanked me, but it was a subdued party that left the town.

They were feeling pretty mouldy after their night out, and I was miserable that the trip was coming to an end. I had enjoyed every minute of it from the moment I had made up my mind to trust the three of them, and we had had such fun. I think they had enjoyed it too; it was horrid to think that I would never see them again, but I cheered myself with the thought that if we had seen much more of each other we would probably have been bored stiff. When we stopped for lunch I did them proud and stood them a splendid lunch with a couple of rounds of rice which put new heart into them.

The trip petered out at Kiating. We dropped the soldiers off at the barracks as we passed and Li came to the mission with me, but everyone was in such a tearing rush arranging the farewell party for Mr. Jones that I said good-bye to Li much more hurriedly than I had intended. Fortunately I managed to slip him a bigger tip than the Crams had planned for him.

All I can remember of the farewell dinner was the expressions on the faces of the guests when Mr. Jones said in his farewell speech: "Heaven will not feel right to me if there are no tea-shops there."

CHAPTER SIXTEEN
WINTER SHOES IN SPRINGTIME

NEXT morning I was rather disappointed to find that Mr. Jones's arrangements for me to share his junk had been altered by the Crams who felt that this plan did not set a good moral example to the Chinese; they had hired the smallest and cheapest junk they could find and it was to trail along behind his. I got into it and remained modestly hidden while all the good-byes were said, but as soon as the junks were round the first bend in the river and out of sight of the mission house, my junk was hauled up alongside his and I transferred to the big one, my little junk just being kept as my bedroom.

It was a delightful way of travelling. We went along with the river, helped by a sail when the wind was right, otherwise the big steering sweep was used as a scull. After all the walking, it was lovely to lie on a kind of bamboo sofa and watch the river bank unroll and listen to a story about each place we passed. Although the stories were fantastic, they were true, and each time we stopped I was introduced to some of the people who had taken part in them.

The weather was perfect, and the welcoming crowds at even the tiniest villages were enormous, but the sadness underlying it all was impossible to miss. Not only was Mr. Jones being exiled from all he loved best in life but the Chinese who came to see him were losing a friend they would never be able to replace. It was the end of an era for them; no longer would they be Szechuanese in a province run by one warlord after another — they were being absorbed into a nation. There was no place now for another Mr. Jones.

When he had first come out to China as a young man he was up in the north and had managed to get through the Boxer Rebellion disguised as a Chinese, and he seemed to have enjoyed every minute of it. As soon as he arrived in China he felt he belonged, and before the rebellion began he had already grown a pigtail. I am not quite sure whether all the missionaries grew them at this time or if he was an exception. Anyway, it helped to disguise him, for when the Chinese pulled it and found that it was genuine, they thought he must be genuine too. After that he was sent to Szechuan, where he was cut off by the warlords from any directives from mission headquarters so that he had lived on his own and developed his own way of spreading the gospel — by example.

As there were practically no roads, the Min River was the main artery; the richest towns were on its banks and, therefore, the warlords fought most of their battles on one side of the river or the other.

As the Chinese proverb "He who strikes the first blow has lost the argument" implies, they do not really like fighting and prefer to spend days in negotiation. When a warlord decided to attack a city, he would advance his troops in a slow, leisurely way towards it, brutally beating up any villages that lay between him and the city. This was calculated to terrify the town into offering a large bribe to be spared the horrors that had been inflicted on the villages. When the army finally arrived at the outskirts of the town, the real bargaining would begin.

It was a very delicate business to strike the bargain between what the town could pay and what the warlord hoped he could keep for himself after he had satisfied the demands of his troops. Naturally the man who presented the town's terms to the warlord was a most important person. He had to be strictly honest and also very brave, for if the offered price was much too low, the warlord would start attacking while the bargaining was going on and the go-between would then be under fire as he was carrying the next offer to the enemy.

Somehow Mr. Jones had become the best go-between for the towns, and until recently — up to the opening of the Chengtu road — any town threatened by a warlord at once sent for Mr. Jones. The warlords liked and trusted him too, and when he assured them that the town really could not pay another cent they would believe him and take the sum offered.

It was not only money that was involved. There were the sacking terms. Originally, a warlord came and captured a town, taking the money while his troops, in lieu of pay, systematically sacked it, raping the women and looting the houses. Then this was found to be too extreme, for the towns were unable to recover, which meant that eventually there would be no towns to sack, and this in turn meant that the warlord would have to go and fight another warlord for his district. Nobody liked that idea at all: it was too much like real war; the chances of being killed were too high, and so was the price of ammunition and equipment. So each warlord kept to his own area, like a man-eating tiger, and visited his victims in turn, allowing them time to recover from a siege before tackling them again.

Mr. Jones was a very moral man, but he was also practical; he knew that to deny Chinese troops any rape at all would obviously be a hopeless job, so he faced up to the fact while making one important stipulation: so long as he was representing a town he made it clear that the soldiers were strictly forbidden to rape virgins. He would have all the virgins rounded up and put in a building where he would be responsible for them himself, and in all the years he was acting for these towns his reputation was such that he had never lost a virgin. No matter how unruly the soldiery might be, they respected his orders.

As we went down the river, he would stop at these towns and meet some of the city fathers who had arranged the terms of surrender. There was only one town where Mr. Jones sadly remarked, as we sailed gently up to the landing stage, "I only managed to save the virgins here; all the married women had to go." The married women were graded by age, income and number of children, and even for the Chinese it seemed rather a curious medium of exchange for a business deal. Even at this town we were given a tremendous welcome; none of the married women seemed to have borne a grudge.

I had heard the same words called out in almost the same tone of voice, and with the same laugh or smile, at nearly all the places where we had stopped so far, and I could now recognize the Chinese for "Why, when you should be growing a beard, have you taken instead a young concubine?" Mr. Jones's reply varied from place to place, so I never did find out what he actually said, but it always brought roars of laughter so I was not at all sure that it was complimentary to me.

We were always escorted by a huge crowd; Mr. Jones walked in front with the high officials and I came afterwards with some of the more junior staff. They would take us to a restaurant and regale us with a huge meal, but as it drew to an end the gaiety would die away and the old men would ask sadly, "Why do you have to go?"

In a country where the expectation of life is so short, to grow old at all was a considerable feat; even if you had done nothing else in your life you became a person of considerable influence once you reached the age of 60. And here was this famous foreigner who was looked up to and deeply loved by everybody on both sides of the Min River, and he was being removed by the mission from his job at exactly the time in his life when he had reached the age where he could carry the most influence.

So the return walk to the junks was always an ordeal, the older ones knowing that it was their final farewell, and what with the emotion and the over-eating I was almost relieved when we reached Suifu on the Yangtze.

At Suifu we went to a Baptist mission run by the American Baptists. The missionaries there were a jolly family with three children. Their standard of living seemed higher than at the other missions I had been in, but as they missed a lot of comforts they had had at home they derived great moral support from the feeling that they were spreading the gospel while living a life of great hardship.

The rest of our journey was on the Yangtze and we were going to travel on a river steamer. I arranged to go early in the morning by myself to the steamer; Mr. Jones, anyway, would be having an official farewell where I would be out of place.

During my previous journeys I had noticed how the Chinese had watched me and discussed me, so I asked Mr. Jones to pretend not to know me at the start of the journey so that he could tell me later on what he heard them say about me. I bought my ticket and went on board where I found a corner on one side of a deck-locker and staked my claim to it by putting down my rucksack and *baifu*; then I watched the farewell to Mr. Jones. I thought that it lacked some of the verve of the farewells on the Min River, but perhaps that was because there were other foreigners present.

As soon as the steamer left, I went back to my little bit of deck-space and unpacked my stuff and arranged my bedding to make myself as comfortable as I could. In no time there was an interested crowd around me, looking at my things and making all kinds of remarks, and I was glad to see Mr. Jones hovering unobtrusively in the background. As foreigners in China always talk to each other when they meet outside the big cities, it would have looked odd if we had not talked, so after about half an hour I went over to where he was sitting in state on a camp-bed and asked what they had said.

"She has been very rich and lost all her money," he replied. "All she has left are the camera and the alarm clock. She probably had a rich husband who grew tired of her as she had no children, or perhaps he died, and now she is very poor, so poor that she has to wear men's winter shoes in springtime."

This was the first time I realized that there was any difference between women's shoes and men's; to me they looked exactly the same, with their cotton uppers and their soles made of cotton rags stitched together in a wodge about half an inch thick. They looked rather like unsmart bedroom slippers and were the most comfortable shoes I have ever worn. I had always bought men's shoes as there was no hope of getting my feet into the women's tiny sizes, and as for seasonal shoes I had no idea they had such things. I always bought half a dozen pairs of shoes at a time, for their one drawback was that they wore out so fast. I was really quite touched by this report; it meant that the Chinese had been so kind to me because they were sorry for me and certainly not from any hope of gain. "Winter shoes in springtime" was apparently a sure sign that I was absolutely down-and-out. Even Mr. Jones seemed sorry for me and when the boat stopped at a village he suggested going ashore and having a meal. I was not feeling very well but thought it would be a good idea, so off we went. It seemed queer to be on our own after the friendly crowds on the Min River. We ambled along until we found a nice little tea-shop. We did not have very much to eat, but when the rinse-water came round I automatically took a big mouthful, rinsed vigorously, and spat out on the floor. Mr. Jones bent forward, looked startled, and then said in a rather wistful voice, "I've been 40 years in China and I've never done that."

We walked back to the boat which was whistling urgently to summon its passengers, and I went and lay down on my bag and dozed. I thought I must be overtired, although it seemed odd, for the junk trip down the river had been like a luxury cruise after the terrific rush up Mount Omei.

That evening I did not feel like eating, and Mr. Jones and I sat silently together watching the river bank go by. The way he seemed to be sucking in these last familiar sights was heart-breaking.

Next day went by in a sort of haze. I thought I had a temperature, but as I was going as fast as possible towards the only doctors and hospitals within reach, there was nothing to be done about it. I told Mr. Jones I was tired and spent the day lying down and drinking delicious Chinese tea.

It was late when we came to Chungking. There was a delegation to meet Mr. Jones, so we parted rather hurriedly and I hired a coolie to take my bundles and staggered up the steps from the river to the mission resthouse. I had written and told them I would be arriving on the boat, so though everybody was in bed, the night-watchman was expecting me and showed me to a room where I simply collapsed on the bed fully dressed.

The night passed in a muddle of dreams or waking nightmares; I was too ill to know which, and at one moment I seemed to hear the voice of a friend in Hong Kong saying, "It's not safe to travel alone, you are bound to get syphilis." And when I woke to find my pillow stuck to my face with a discharge from my throat, I began to imagine things. As soon as it was getting light, I tottered downstairs and took a rickshaw to the mission hospital. Early though it was, there was already a long queue and I tailed onto it, leaning against the wall. Once a nurse came out with a patient, and when she saw me there she beckoned me to come up to the surgery. The doctor, a tall, thin, tired man, told me to sit down and said, "What can I do for you?"

"I've got syphilis."

"I think we had better take a test before deciding," he said gently. And a few minutes later he told me, "There's no need to worry; it's a bad attack of tonsillitis."

They were very kind and arranged for a Chinese nurse to come to the mission house until my temperature went down. They got a rickshaw to take me back and just as I was leaving, the doctor put his hand on my arm, smiled and said, "It doesn't matter what other people have told you, there is still only one way to get syphilis."

164

As soon as I knew what was the matter with me I began to feel almost cured. And next day when some people whom I had met on my first visit to Chungking came to ask me to stay with them, I fairly leapt out of bed.

Hugh and Anne had a lovely house on the other side of the river, and in it was a fascinating house-trained white cockatoo called Joe. He would arrive on your shoulder, muttering hoarsely; he would give your ear a friendly nibble and then sidle away to the nearest piece of newspaper and relieve himself, before coming back for another chat. Every room had its quota of newspaper, as he needed one every 20 minutes. I could have watched him for hours, with his serious air, hoarse-voiced remarks and unfailing aim.

"How on earth did you train him?" I asked.

"Oh," said Anne, matter-of-factly, "just like a dog. Rubbed his beak in it and smacked him."

It was a lovely change for me to lie in bed, in clean sheets, in a big room of my own, with a nice *amah* to wash and iron my things, and a restful mental atmosphere where nothing was taken too seriously. There was no worrying about lost souls, or failing in one's duty; smoking and drinking were regarded as a normal part of life, like aimless conversation and silly jokes.

In the evenings we would sit on the verandah with iced drinks and literally watch Chungking burn. But from this house across the river it was a much more dramatic sight than I had had on my earlier visit, when I could see much less and my impressions were almost confined to the smell of smoke and the sound of shouts and cries. It was a lovely sight, with the flames shooting brightly up across the river against the background of hills. But it was horrifying that we could sit so safely and watch as a mere spectacle hundreds of homes burning and that we could do nothing about it. China was like that, and at times it was just too much for me.

Chungking was overcrowded with refugees and they had no water except what was carried up from the river by coolies and sold by the pint; a drought had been going on for months and the only form of lighting in the refugees' homes — which had been knocked together out of cardboard cartons, paper and old sacks — were cotton wicks laid in a bath of oil. There could be only one result, and there it was before our eyes nearly every night of the week that I stayed with Hugh and Anne.

165

In order to stay sane, the mind had to reject the normal reaction to such a sight. Of course, we gave old clothes and money to help, but even then with the feeling that by the time it trickled down through the various channels there would be nothing left for the people we had meant it for.

It was odd how I had longed for luxury and now when I had had it for only two or three days I was already thinking nostalgically of sleeping on floors with bugs in my bed. It certainly took me more than three days to tire of them.

CHAPTER SEVENTEEN

A New Scar on an Old Face

THE next part of my journey was going to be the most interesting, as I should be breaking new ground. Chiang Kai-shek had been building a number of new roads, for he knew how important it would be to have roads into French Indo-China and Burma if the Japanese cut him off from the coast. The new road to Kunming, the railhead for Indo-China, was nearly finished; indeed some people said it was quite finished, but nobody seemed very certain. Buses went off in that direction but no European had actually gone all the way on a bus, so I was unable to find out what it was going to be like — not that it mattered if the bus could not take me all the way, because I love walking. Merely to put one foot in front of the other gives me great pleasure, so I was half hoping that the road would not be finished all the way. Another slight complication was that the British Consul was supposed to have said at a cocktail party that no British subject would be allowed to go on that route alone because someone had been kidnapped there recently and he naturally did not want to be responsible for any more of his subjects getting into trouble.

I always prefer not to ask for permission if there is the slightest chance of it being refused, because it makes it more difficult to do what you want. As a precaution against kidnapping I had a beautiful document written in the best Chinese calligraphy to certify that I was extremely poor, had no money, and absolutely no one would want to ransom me. Then I took all the money I had, except for a few shillings for bus fares and food, to the Chungking Post Office and arranged to have it sent to the post office in

Kunming. This ensured that any Chinese who might be interested in me as a possible source of cash could easily find out that I would be unable to produce any more until I had safely reached Kunming. Then, in case the story of what the consul had said was true, I told everyone, including Anne, that I would leave two days later than I actually intended.

After all these precautions I relaxed and left the rest to chance. Then, as we were going to bed one night, I told Anne that I would be catching the bus next morning. She was delighted with this cloak-and-dagger attitude and tiptoed off to bed. At six next morning in the chilly dawn, my heart began to sink; I had no breakfast because my departure had been kept a secret from the servants, and this also meant that I had to lug my stuff down the hill till I found a coolie asleep by the side of the road.

The bus did not leave till seven and I had half an hour to buy my ticket. With my conversation card for "Please give me a ticket to ..." at the ready, I joined the queue for the ticket office. When I reached the window I held up the card and said "Kunming", but instead of my ticket there was a volley of Chinese, the only part of which I could understand was "Not Kunming!"

I tried to stay and argue the point but the crowd behind me pushed me out of the way. At first I thought that perhaps I had gone to the wrong window, but it was the only one and everybody who was not too busy to talk to me seemed to be going to Kunming too, and they all waved me back to the same inhospitable window. By this time I had wasted ten minutes and the queue was now twice as long as when I had first joined it. After an agonizing wait, there I was back at the same window with my card in my hand and "Kunming" on my lips, only to be met by exactly the same volley of Chinese, with no words I could recognize except "Not Kunming!" I was given an even more vigorous shove from behind and I was on my own again.

Almost crying with vexation I rushed round to the tail of the queue again, having wasted a further 15 minutes, and watched at least 30 people who seemed to be going to Kunming buy their tickets with no trouble at all. I now tried to persuade the people next to me in the queue to help me in my plight and stumbled along in Chinese using all my cards in my desperation. "Please wake me up in time to catch the bus" and "Does this bus go to..." made a good start. My neighbours thought this was great fun and seized the rest of my cards and started passing them round. I was afraid that "I do not rejoice in soup" and "I have no money" might confuse the issue, but they were so taken with the cards that they became very friendly, and by the time I turned up at the ticket office for the third time they had made me understand that, unlike the other buses I had travelled on before where I could buy a ticket to my final destination no matter how many days' journey it was away, on this trip they only sold tickets for one day's run. The man ahead of me nobly waited and told the office-clerk the name of the town at which my bus would stop that night, while I held up "Please give me a ticket to..." Even then it seemed like magic when the ticket actually appeared through the opening.

All this delay had lost me any chance of getting a seat in the bus, which had already started its engine, but once the Chinese start to help you, nothing can stop them, and my two new friends hurled themselves on the driver and prevented him from putting the engine in gear, while another, inspired by their aggressive spirit, threw my baggage through a broken window and gave my bottom such a shove as I was fighting my way in through the door that I shot half-way down the middle of the bus and came to rest on a pile of luggage, where I thankfully stayed. Through the window I could see my helpers rush off to fight their way into their own bus, but I did not see how they made out, for the moment they let go of our driver he let in the clutch and thundered off.

We had started on the opposite side of the river from Chungking, so it was not long before we were right out in the country, and the road would not have been considered finished in any country but China. Behind us an impenetrable wall of dust hid everything from view. We passed through no towns of any size, so I supposed the road must be following quite a different route from the old pony-and-coolie track. The tea-shops at the bus halts were miserable little places, but the food there was as good as ever. We made pretty good time, for all the passengers were going all the way so that there were none of the usual delays while endless small bundles or screaming livestock were ferreted out of the mound of baggage at wayside stops. The bus itself was fairly new — it still had some bits of broken glass in some of the windows — and the road was too new for its surface to be badly holed yet.

I was very glad when we came at last to a fair-sized town and the bus pulled up for the night, for I was shockingly soft after my tonsillitis and a week's luxury staying with Anne. But despite the size of the town I failed to find a hotel, so I tried asking for the postmaster, as I had heard that many postmasters spoke English. My coolie seemed to get the idea at once, started off in great style, and led me to a house in a small side street. I knocked and, sure enough, I was greeted in English: the coolie had taken me to the mission.

The young man who opened the door to me was a European in Chinese dress; he seemed a bit disconcerted at my sudden arrival, and I cannot say I was altogether surprised, but he invited me in. Mr. Chad was the head of the mission, and with him were his wife and twin sons. They were Australians and they had another Australian missionary staying with them. Mrs. Chad seemed genuinely pleased to see another foreign woman and they asked me to stay the night. Fortunately I had arrived just in time for supper, at which meal they talked nothing but shop. Everything was so simple for them. They sincerely believed they had received the "Call" direct from God to come and tell the Chinese about Christianity.

"Such a field," said Mr. Chad. "Millions of souls to be saved. We must work night and day to spread the gospel so that they can go to Heaven."

"What happens to those who do not have a chance of hearing you?" I asked. "Do they go to Hell?"

"I do not think so," he replied. "It is only those who have the chance and reject it who are not forgiven."

This seemed to me to mean that for every convert there must be at least 200 souls who were condemned to everlasting fire. But this appalling thought did not seem to disturb them in the least, and I hardly liked to point it out to them. I must have betrayed something by my expression because as soon as the meal was over, Mrs. Chad, with various little nods and winks, persuaded the men to leave us alone. Then she drew her chair near mine and said, "Do you feel you would like to tell me anything? Do you need any help?"

"Thank you very much, but I am really enjoying myself, and your having me to stay like this is a tremendous help."

She looked disappointed and it was obviously not the answer she had hoped for because she started to tell me about her life in Australia before she got the "Call".

"I was working in the mantle department in one of Melbourne's biggest stores," she said. "I've seen Life. I've smoked and been to cinemas."

It was difficult to imagine what the highly civilized Chinese made of her.

Next morning we were up early. During grace before breakfast I was startled to hear Mr. Chad say, "Please, Lord, help our guest to get a seat in the bus."

But they did not leave it entirely to the Lord; the two men came with me to the bus station, and when I saw the crowd round the bus I understood the need for prayer. It looked as if 200 people were trying to force their way into the bus. Mr. Chad and his friend rolled up their sleeves and stood in front of me.

"Hold on to us," they said. "No matter what happens, don't let go."

With heads down and fists flailing, we charged the crowd and used our combined weight in so determined a manner that it gave way before us. As soon as we reached the door of the bus they got on either side of me and heaved me in. I pushed my way to the back and leant out of a window and thanked them very much.

"Don't thank us. Thank the Lord," said Mr. Chad, without a smile. "We will leave you now as we have much to do."

And they turned and walked off.

After we left the town we could see the road stretching ahead like a new scar on an old face. When we drove through the few small villages without stopping, hordes of dogs — big fine ones, with heavy coats like chows — came rushing out of them, and you could tell from the frenzy of their barking that buses were still a novelty. They would dash snapping at the wheels, black, white and brown, in a tight bunch; the driver would swerve and accelerate; there would be a bump as the bus hit one of them, and then a ghastly scream as the rest of them closed round it to tear it apart. Luckily we did not go through many villages, but although the same thing happened at each one, I could not make out whether the driver was trying to avoid them or hit them with his sudden swerves.

We were gradually climbing now through queer barren country, with the road winding in wild curves that had been cut in the hillside by men with picks and shovels. The whole length of the road between Chungking and Kunming had been made by hand, and it seemed odd that after all this toil there was no traffic but us, as we rushed along with the empty road ahead and behind. I missed the squeaking of wheelbarrows and all the coolies bearing their carrying-poles, with pigs and chickens dangling at either end; it all seemed unnatural.

The town we came to that night was very small, but it had a government resthouse, converted out of an old temple, where the bus stopped. I arranged with the driver that I would leave my rucksack on the bus overnight, as I hoped it would constitute some sort of claim on a seat in the morning.

I walked round the town, for there was still some daylight left, and I saw a lot of lively conscripts, but I could not make out whether they were soldiers or labour battalions. The women in the streets nearly all had bound feet, and this was the first place where I had seen more feet bound than unbound. Only the girls of 16 or less had normal, unbound feet. It seemed to me that now they had given up binding their feet they had lost all pride in them.The other women, even the ancient grandmothers, showed that they still thought their tiny feet were their biggest attraction, for no matter how ragged their clothes, the little shoes were always in beautiful condition and were embroidered in bright silk with flowers, butterflies or a bat for luck; whereas the girls with normal feet had the most deplorable-looking shoes and stockings, even when they were otherwise quite smartly dressed.

It was dark when I returned to the inn, and as a party of soldiers drinking in the hall already seemed to be pretty merry, I thought it best to lock the door when I went to bed. I must have been asleep for an hour or so when I was woken up by someone trying to open the door. I sat up and shouted "No!" in my clearest Chinese. There was no answer, just dead silence, and then a little whispering, followed by retreating footsteps. I lay down triumphant, but only for a minute or two; then I heard a new noise against the window, the top part of which was open. There was some muffled giggling, and in through the window came a policeman's hat on the end of a long stick. It turned round and did a kind of bow and was withdrawn, and a voice called out for my papers.

So I got up and let the policeman in. He turned out to be as nice as his manner of announcing himself and, seeing I was in bed, he said I could stay there. If I let him take my passport to the police station I could stay in bed and he would bring it back in the morning before the bus started. I jumped at the idea, for I thought that if I had a policeman with me I would have no difficulty in getting a seat. So I called in a lordly way for a pot of tea, and we sipped and smiled and bowed. Then he wrapped the passport carefully up in a piece of oiled paper and left, making certain that I locked the door behind him.

Next morning I made the acquaintance of the worst lavatory I had met in China. When I asked where it was I was shown a large bamboo wall with a small door at one side. The smell, of course, was appalling, but I was used to that by now. Inside was a large square pit, full right up almost to the edge of the wall, and across this ghastly pool were some miserable bits of wood on which one was supposed to balance. I crept a little way out over that seething mass and I still think that this was the bravest thing I have ever done, especially as just as I was about to leave, a large basket on the end of a pole suddenly arrived over the wall and scooped up a lot of precious fertilizer, nearly tipping me into the pit as it did so. I was sweating with fright, for I felt that if I had fallen in, there would have been nothing for it but suicide. I extricated myself and escaped out of the door, only to find several of the other passengers kindly waiting till I had finished. This showed typical Chinese tact, for although they did not mind company in the lavatory, they realized that I probably would.

The policeman was waiting at the hotel. He gave me back my passport and then, as I had hoped, escorted me to the bus and not only cleared a way through the mob but made quite sure I was comfortably settled in my seat. All day we travelled through the barren countryside, and here the road was so new that they were actually working on it; thousands of people were carrying one little basket on their heads or two on a carrying-pole.

It was a great relief that the road did not pass through any villages, so no more dogs were killed. When we reached the top of the pass there was a sudden change. We joined onto an old road which led down into Kunming, and a lovely green oasis it looked. High up on a nearby hill there were crowds of pilgrims on their way to visit a monastery, and the road in front of the bus was crowded with coolies, wheelbarrows and sedan chairs. We were back in the old familiar China again.

In Kunming I stayed with a man and his wife who ran the sewage farm. It gave me endless satisfaction to watch the lovely clear water running off to fertilize the fields. When I thought of the ghastly pit I had so nearly fallen into, it seemed like the greatest discovery of the age that such a simple process could make such a tremendous transformation.

Now I had to make up my mind which way to go on from here. There were two alternatives: I could go on by bus, north-west to Tali and along the old tribute road to Myitkyina or Bhamo, or I could go south by rail into Indo-China and visit Angkor Wat. By both routes I could end up in Burma. Wholeheartedly I wanted to go north-west towards the high mountains and to cross the three great rivers — the Mekong, the Salween and the Irrawaddy — before they ran down into the low country and became domesticated. Moreover, I wanted to walk instead of sitting in a bus or train.

"I want to sleep out-of-doors," I told my host, "and not to be bothered by the lavatory problem."

"Ah," he replied, darkly, "there will be pigs, then."

This was not the first time I had heard of the pigs, but at that moment I did not feel like pursuing the subject.

The first thing to do was to get permission through the British Consul to go by bus as far as Tali, and I had already met cries of "No women allowed alone!" from most of the people I met. So off I went to see the consul. He lived in a lovely house with a beautiful moon-door. I did not have to wait; a servant took my card and showed me into the office, and the consul came out to me at once.

"How do you do," he said. "I hear you want to go to Tali?"

I was terribly relieved he had only mentioned Tali and not Burma, for once I could get to Tali there was not likely to be anyone there to stop me from going on. So I said in what seemed to me a very downright and convincing manner, "I just want to go and see the town and the lake; then I was thinking I would come back and have a look at Angkor Wat."

He smiled. "That would be a lovely trip," he said. "Give me your passport and I will have it stamped for Tali. Then you must come and have dinner with us tomorrow night and meet my wife."

I left the consulate very pleased at the Machiavellian way I had managed things. Next day I went to dinner and to collect my passport. The consul himself was in the courtyard by the moon-door; he took me into a big living-room where he introduced me to his wife.

"This is the lady I was telling you about who is going to walk into Burma," he said, taking all the wind out of my sails at once.

But they were both so nice to me that in no time I forgot how silly I had been and enjoyed one of the happiest evenings in my life. Their house was so beautiful and it was furnished with a perfect mixture of English and Chinese things. The lighting was soft and attractive and encouraged confidences, so it was past two in the morning before I left.

Next day I was out early looking for a bus. There was not a regular service; someone with a bus or a lorry would look round for goods or people, and when he was satisfied that he had collected as much as his vehicle could possibly carry, he would start. I found a lorry taking mixed freight: mostly goods, with a few people to sit on top. As I was a foreigner I had to pay extra and take the seat in the cab with the driver. He was starting next day, which was a great piece of luck, and I was excited at the thought that I should soon be walking again and on a road which had been the regular route by which tribute had been sent from Burma for thousands of years.

Back at the sewage farm I found two missionaries had come to ask if I could take a package to the missionaries in Tali. It was fairly large and I think it must have been a piece of furniture. They had been waiting for months to find someone who could take it there.

The start next morning was much more dignified than it would have been with any of the buses. People did not seem to be anxious to go to Tali; there were only four other passengers. This was not surprising, for the lorry was uncovered at the back and the four men were perched on top of the tarpaulin that covered the freight and had nothing to hang onto but the ropes it was tied down with. I was not very much more comfortable, as the cab was only made for two, and the driver's mate had to sit with us next to the door so that he could leap out quickly and give the engine first-aid in moments of crisis. The road was appalling from the start; it was not wide enough for a lorry and it looked as if the lorry drivers themselves had tried to enlarge it, it was so haphazardly done. The scenery was grand, with steep mountains and fast rivers.

Fright seems to sharpen all my senses, and everything around me, scenery, people, animals, noise, temperature and light. I can take them all in and have a photographic impression of a moment of fear that I can never forget. It was not long after we started that such a moment arrived.

I was listening to the driver and his mate talking, and I had the impression that they were worried about a river. It was not raining and there had been no sudden change in the temperature to cause floods, so I was wondering what risk this river could entail when we rounded a sharp corner and saw a river some 200 feet almost vertically below us. The road sloped down along the cliff-face and the outer edge had slipped a little so the lorry ran along at a sickening tilt. Across the river I could see the road climbing away up the other bank, and I wondered how we would cross to it. Then I saw a swinging chain bridge that looked so frail I thought it must be for coolie traffic only, but as we came nearer I saw that the road stopped by the bridge, and I took a quick look at the driver's face. He was not happy; he changed down to low gear and muttered to his mate.

The ornamental part of the bridge was pretty enough; there was the usual attractive wooden structure with a sloping roof, like so many other Chinese bridges, but between it and the other gateway on the other side of the river there were merely some heavy chains with planks lying across them. No doubt they had all been good sound planks when first they were laid, but that was years ago and they had not been touched since. Some were broken and some were missing. They might once have been fastened to the chains, but there were no fastenings now. And over this bridge the driver drove his lorry. The loose planks jumped up ahead of us as we came, and the whole bridge bucked and swayed so that I wondered how the outside passengers managed to hold on and was reminded of happier days at fun-fairs.

The lorry stopped when we reached solid ground. The passengers climbed down from their perch on the back and stood in a little group, looking at the bridge in perfect silence. I wondered what they thought: a Hindu would have believed that our survival was pre-ordained — it had already been settled whether the lorry went into the river so nothing he could do would affect his fate; a Muslim would have said a prayer and then left it all to Allah, so if we had gone in it would have been an act of spite on Allah's part. But what did the Chinese think? I had no idea.

One of the other passengers came and spoke to me. At first I could not understand what he was saying, but then I realized that he was speaking English.

"No good," he said, putting a great deal of meaning into this bare understatement.

I never discovered how he came to know English, for no matter how slowly I spoke I could not make him understand one word, so he could answer no questions. However, he had quite a good vocabulary of his own and could tell me anything he thought might be interesting.

We bounded and slid along all day, and I found the scenery was so lovely and so varied that the discomfort hardly mattered. We crossed some enchanting little bridges spanning brooks; they consisted only of a couple of enormous stone slabs and beautiful carved stone balustrades. There was only an inch or so to spare on each side, and it was heartbreaking to see the balustrades so chipped and broken by the lorries and buses. Some of them had been knocked right off and lay in the stream, blocking up the watercourse and making it spread out and cut away the banks. The villages had not altered for centuries, for no modernization had reached this remote district yet. They all had roofed or stone gateways, and every street was paved with the same enormous blocks that were used on the little bridges. I envied Marco Polo who had seen this magnificent country at the height of its prosperity, when all the roads were kept in first-class repair so that the tribute from the outlying dependencies could come quickly and safely to the capital.

We stopped at small tea-houses built of bamboo and roofed over with leaves, and my English-speaking friend would be the centre of admiration as he translated the menu for me. The driver would sit down with us, for he showed no disposition to hurry on and sometimes a passenger had to persuade him to get moving again. Here in the south-west corner of China everything seemed so peaceful; the undeclared war with Japan was far away and there was none of the tension in the air that I had felt at Chungking.

Then the lorry turned a corner and stopped. There, on the road, a large and unusually smart car had broken down. A nervous-looking bespectacled man came over and asked the driver for help. We all tumbled out and walked over to have a look. The rest of the passengers were ahead of me, talking and laughing until suddenly they fell silent, turned round as one man and walked back. As soon as they passed me I could see what had upset them: sitting on the wall on the other side of the car were three

Japanese in European dress; two of them wore breeches and riding-boots, and all of them were so strung with revolvers, cameras, thermos-flasks, each in its highly polished leather case, that one could see little of them but their faces. For a moment we stared at each other speechless with astonishment, then one of them looked as if he was going to speak so I quickly turned back to the lorry. The others had been watching me, and as soon as they saw me coming back they all broke into smiles. "All bad, Japanese army mans," said my English-speaking friend, and then, rounding on the unfortunate bespectacled Chinese, added in a tone of withering scorn, "No good man, either."

The wretched man became even more nervous and fairly writhed at this abuse. It turned out that he was the interpreter employed by these Japanese and now that the car had broken down he was trying to persuade our driver and mate to mend it. But they so loathed the Japanese that this was the last thing they wanted to do. Eventually, after a long, threatening harangue, the interpreter prevailed upon them and they went to work while the poor interpreter stood by himself, shunned equally by us and by the Japanese.

As soon as they had the engine running again, the driver and mate came rushing back to the lorry and got under way almost before the passengers had time to climb on the back. The Japanese were hurrying too, for whoever was last would be stuck behind the other vehicle in a cloud of dust unless they were content to dawdle along a couple of miles behind. The Japanese had a large and powerful car which could obviously go much faster than our lorry, so if we could get away ahead of them we could annoy them much more than they could annoy us. There was no need to explain this to the passengers on the lorry; they understood at once and shouted with triumph as we scraped past the car. At first the Japanese tried to overtake us, but our driver would have none of that and the road was so bad that it was quite impossible for them to overtake without his full co-operation. So they had to suffer our dust and exhaust for three hours or so, when we drew up at a couple of small bamboo tea-houses.

We piled out and sat round a table, congratulating ourselves on having so ably insulted the Japanese, when we heard their car arriving. They too pulled up; the two generals in their polished boots got out and spoke bossily to the interpreter who went into the next tea-house. We could see him through the gaps in the wall, feverishly dusting the tables and chairs; then the generals arrived, and finally the A.D.C., who unshipped one of his thermoses and gave it to the proprietor so that he could use their own official water for making their tea. Then the A.D.C. picked up the tea-cups, carried them outside, and began washing them very ostentatiously with hot water out of yet another thermos. Our passengers watched this ridiculous performance with mounting rage, and the English-speaker turned to me.

"What bad word in Japanese?" he asked.

I dimly remembered my brother had told me that *baka*, which means roughly "bloody fool", was the rudest thing you could call a Japanese, and it had stuck in my mind.

"*Baka!*" I yelled in a loud, clear voice.

There was a moment's shocked silence from the other tea-house, and I knew I had hit the target. The rest of the passengers were eager for more abuse. I could think of none, but we managed well enough. I shouted "Tokyo!" and then all the passengers chanted "*Baka!*" in unison.

Again there was silence from the other tea-house, followed by a brisk order in Japanese and the wretched interpreter appeared, presumably to ask us to behave ourselves. But he never had a chance to speak; everyone shouted at him and shook their fists until he ran back into the tea-house faster than he had come out.

The passengers turned to me in fits of laughter. "More!" they cried.

So I went on calling out the names of all the Japanese towns I could remember and, after each one, they would all yell, "*Baka!*" at the tops of their voices.

I was beginning to run out of towns when the Japanese ran out of patience and got up and left before the man in the tea-shop had had time to make their tea. We watched in deathly stillness as they passed, and as soon as they had driven off we all solemnly stood up and bowed to each other. For a moment I completely forgot that I was not Chinese.

That night we stopped at what looked like a country farmhouse. I think the people must have been friends or relations of the driver's for he slept in the house, but the passengers did not go indoors and must have been put up in an outhouse. Fortunately I was invited in and the story of our encounter with the Japanese went down very well. The farmer and his wife and daughter were in fits of laughter. As the driver gave them a blow-by-blow account, they kept turning to me and saying, "Good! Good!"

I slept upstairs, in a store-room without a bed. The daughter showed me the lavatory, the pleasantest I had yet seen apart from those on the boats. It was an extension of the verandah, and directly underneath were a fine big sow and a litter of healthy piglets.

Next morning the daughter came and woke me up with a lovely bowl of hot gruel. When I tried to pay, they would not take a penny, so I lined them up and took their photographs. The driver wrote the address on an envelope in Chinese and when I had had the film developed in Burma I sent off the photograph to them. I hope they got it.

Next morning it was an enchanting spring day; the sky was a wonderful blue with small white clouds but not a grain of dust in the air, and the country looked pastoral and happy. Once, when the lorry was stopped, I saw a coolie coming down the road with a carrying-pole and an enormous basket dangling from either end. He was moving with the coolie's invariable jog-trot which is supposed to jump the pole up and down and somehow halve the weight. As he came nearer I heard a cheerful and vaguely familiar noise which grew louder and louder until I recognized it and realized that he was carrying two big baskets of baby chicks. This part of China was full of fowls and even the smallest villages had their hatcheries. That morning it was one of those days when everything seems perfect, but after lunch a slight cloud appeared when the driver's mate began to suffer very badly from wind. In the end the driver and I turned him out of the cab and made him ride on the bonnet instead. After that I travelled in luxury and was able to stretch my legs for the first time in two days. And so we crossed over our last little carved-stone bridge and came, not to Tali itself, but to a caravanserai on the main tribute road.

Walking up the street were all kinds of tribesmen from the hills, among them large, laughing Tibetans with their big mules brightly decorated with coloured wools. To the north and west for hundreds of miles were mountains where there was no kind of mechanical transport at all — and indeed hardly even anything on wheels — and where the people were high-spirited and uninhibited. I stood with my baggage at my feet and hardly heard the driver and the passengers say good-bye.

CHAPTER EIGHTEEN
WALKING INTO BURMA

I WISHED I had the courage just to trek off into the mountains, but the hideous spectre of what would happen to me when I ran out of money soon put an end to my dreaming and I turned my attention to getting a room for the night and a coolie for the morning to take me to Tali. To my disgust I realized that the heavy parcel for the mission meant that I would need two coolies.

The Chinese love talking, and if they had nobody else to talk to they would try to talk to me. Although two coolies would be happier than one, it was not so much fun for me, for as soon as they realized how little I could speak they would give me up as a bad job and talk to each other for the rest of the way.

It was another lovely day when I started off with my two coolies. We only had ten miles to go so we should be at Tali by noon; all the same I was impatient, and if it had not been for the mission parcel I think I would not have bothered about Tali and headed straight for the hills. However, it would have been a silly thing to do, for the lake was renowned for its beauty and so was the old town. We walked along in the sunshine, with little spring flowers round our feet, and occasionally crossed small streams on carved marble bridges.

The mountains closed in ahead; they stood in a great semicircle, at the foot of which must lie the lake. We were climbing slightly all the time, and soon the tiled roofs and town wall began to show and we came to a lovely gateway built in two storeys, each with a saucy *retroussé* curve to its roof.

I had been looking forward to the mission, hoping that I should be able to get a bath there and that it would rid me of a mysterious little itch, and when we reached it, the mission was a big surprise. There was a high wall with a tiled top and a fine door with a spirit-screen inside. The door opened onto a wide, clean, empty courtyard, baking in the hot sun. There was nobody there, so the coolies put down their loads and one of them went to find a servant. I suddenly remembered that the note to the mission about the parcel was in my *baifu*, so I squatted down and started to untie it. As I was undoing the knots I heard footsteps and, looking up, I saw a young foreign man in Chinese dress coming down the steps from the house.

"How do you do," he said, with a smile.

But just as I was getting up to shake his hand, a look of horror came over his face. He turned round in a flash, gathered up his gown in one hand and flew back up the steps. At the top he paused long enough to say, "Take that stuff away, we haven't any of those here!" His quivering finger pointed to the white floor of the court-yard, across which a large, well-nourished bedbug, obviously from my bedding, was wandering in search of better quarters.

I squashed it quickly and tied up my bundle. The coolies were regarding the scene with astonishment. Then from the spirit-screen came the sound of an English voice, and round it came a tall, sunburnt man in an Australian felt hat, with a pistol in a holster round his waist and a knife in his belt.

"Hello, what's up?" he said.

"The young man is upset because I've got bedbugs," I answered.

"Never heard of anything so ridiculous." He turned to the young man, who had now been joined by another who was almost identical but a little shorter.

"Has this lady come to stay?" he asked.

Absolutely in unison they cried, "No, she can't stay! We are not married, and Mr. and Mrs. Wallace are away."

"I don't want to stay," I replied. "I only came here to leave this parcel for the Wallaces. If you will take it and this note, I will leave at once."

The man by the gate came up to me. "Wait a minute," he said. "Let's get this straight. My name is Brocklehurst. Where are you going?"

"I'm on my way to Burma and was asked to leave this parcel for the Wallaces as I was coming here to see Tali and the lake. I didn't know that the Wallaces had left."

The two young men, keeping a sharp lookout for bedbugs, now came down the steps and across the courtyard to join us.

"We are sorry," said the second young man. "We cannot ask you to stay because it would look so bad to the Chinese if we had a woman in the mission for the night and Mrs. Wallace is not here. But it is very kind of you to bring this box; I think she has been expecting it for some time. Lunch is ready now, so please come and join us."

I did not know quite what to do. I certainly did not want them to think I was on my dignity about the bedbug, but on the other hand there was no point keeping the coolies hanging round while I had lunch, and I would need one of them to take my baggage on to wherever I eventually decided to spend the night.

"I think I'd better go on," I said. "Otherwise I'll have to find another coolie and it's easier to keep these ones."

Brocklehurst now intervened.

"I'm leaving for Burma too," he said, "and you must come with me; I couldn't possibly let you go by yourself. My man Jimmie has just been fixing up about donkeys and you have so little luggage we can take you on with no trouble."

I was inwardly appalled at this idea, for I had set my heart on doing this last part of my journey by myself. Brocklehurst obviously did not feel as I did about travelling and I was shocked that anybody should travel through someone else's country looking as if he intended to use a revolver if he got into trouble. Moreover, the way he spoke of "my man Jimmie" seemed to strike the wrong note.

"Thank you very much," I said, "but I'm quite all right on my own. I've come this far by myself so I can certainly manage."

He looked really upset. "I couldn't possibly let you go on alone like this. If anything happened — I mean, you might get ill.... Well, anyway, I will not let you go alone, that's definite."

"Well, it's no use standing out here," said one of the young missionaries. "Let's have lunch and discuss things then."

"The coolies..." I began.

"Don't worry about them; Jimmie will look after them," said Brocklehurst. "Hi! Jimmie!"

At the shout, a dear little Chinese came running. He was wearing khaki trousers and a European coat, and he had one of the nicest smiles I have ever seen.

"Jimmie, you fix Missy's coolie," said Brocklehurst and, taking me by the arm, he swept me into the mission dining-room.

During the meal, things became a little clearer. Brocklehurst had just arrived from the eastern border with Tibet where he had been trying to bring back a pair of baby giant pandas alive for the London Zoo. He had been doing this sort of thing all his life; he had been with Shackleton in the Arctic, and had spent several years in Africa and Abyssinia and the Sudan, where he had organized a zoo. He had failed to bring back his pandas and was very upset about it for, owing to some muddle, a baby panda had been killed.

He really seemed to be a very nice man, but he annoyed me by treating me as if I were helpless and delicate, and I had come to pride myself on being neither. But there seemed no way of getting out of travelling with him without appearing as ridiculous as the missionaries who would not let me come into the mission without a chaperone. So we arranged that I would spend the night in the town at an inn and next afternoon we would leave for Burma. Brocklehurst explained this to Jimmie, who took my bags down to the inn while I went off to see what I could of the lake.

I did not appreciate the lake as I should have done. It was a beautiful colour and lay in a most magnificent setting but, after the morning's happenings, my feelings were in such a mixed state that I was not in the right frame of mind for scenery. Natural beauty has to be on a Himalayan scale if it is to annihilate my petty thoughts, and poor Lake Tali, with its gentle beauty, completely failed.

I walked along arguing with myself. It was plain that if I stayed with Brocklehurst I would lose contact with the Chinese; he was older than I and he had been brought up to believe that there were natives and white people and, perhaps as a result of living so much in the Sudan, had never questioned this belief. He did not dislike the natives or treat them unkindly — far from it: he was keen to look after them in a paternalistic way. Indeed, I had a slightly uneasy feeling that perhaps women might also be included among the "lesser breeds". On the other hand, if I went with him, there would be a wonderful opportunity of camping each night in open country, sleeping under the stars, and washing in mountain streams. And I had to admit that it was nice to be treated again as if I were a normal woman and not an unfortunate freak.

Slightly calmed — by the scenery or mere exhaustion, for I had walked a good 15 miles — I went back to Tali. There was Jimmie, sitting by the main gate, waiting to tell me what arrangements he had been able to make. Pretty poor they were too: a bed in a room with two Chinese and one wall open onto the street. The innkeeper must have thought that as they would not have me at the mission there must be something wrong with me.

Next morning I was naturally up bright and early, as I had been practically sleeping in the road, so I started out to do some shopping. Tali and the villages around specialized in making white leather waistcoats with pockets all the way round and sometimes decorated with strips of coloured leather. I bought two of them and then went on to the shoe-shop and bought six pairs of cloth shoes. They still had to be in men's sizes, but this time I insisted on spring ones.

As we were going to camp, I thought it would be fun to have some tobacco for my pipe, which I had not smoked since I had been on Mount Omei. I went into a shop that looked as if it sold tobacco and started a pantomime to explain that I wanted to buy some. This naturally drew a crowd, all anxious to try their hand at interpreting. Things were going very well, and the proprietor had started to bring out his various tobaccos, when Brocklehurst and Jimmie suddenly burst through the crowd.

"What is happening?" asked Brocklehurst anxiously. "Are you all right?"

I thought of the time when I had been frightened of being hemmed in by Chinese and realized with thankfulness how completely my attitude had changed. Now that I was not frightened, I was quite natural with them and they liked me for that. It is a confidence that can only be got by travelling alone; I have never felt in touch with the people in the same way when travelling with another person of my own race. The laughing and arguing crowd fell silent and then drifted away, and by the time I had bought my tobacco there were just a few onlookers in a distant semicircle.

We walked back to the mission where the donkeys were assembled; they were to go with us to Laokai and there we would have to get some more. This would be much quicker than walking, for we would not have to keep to the regular stages.

The missionaries had given Brocklehurst a load to be taken to two lady missionaries in Laokai. So we left. I was walking, Jimmie was riding, and there was a spare donkey besides the loaded ones. I had been very firm about not riding so Brocklehurst was obliged to walk too.

This kind of walking, I soon realized, was going to stretch my leg muscles. We reached the caravanserai where I had left the lorry in a third of the time I had taken, and we swept straight through it without stopping — not even for a cup of tea. But that night by a small camp-fire above a little stream and under the stars made up for the loss of the tea. Jimmie's half-European cooking did not produce nearly such good food as I should have had in an eating-house, but after the exercise I would have eaten anything.

Just before dinner I told Brocklehurst that I was going upstream to have a wash. I put my hand underneath my Chinese gown and undid the pouch with my money, passport and the few valuables I possessed, pulled it off, and laid it on the top of my rucksack.

Brocklehurst watched me in amazement, and as I laid down the pouch he started laughing so hard that I thought he would hurt himself. I waited for the paroxysm to pass and when at last he could speak he pointed at the pouch and gasped, "I thought that it was a baby."

That set me off laughing too, and Jimmie came up to share in the fun.

Now I realized why he had been so firm about not letting me go alone. When he had seen the shape of my figure and the way I had been received at the mission, he had jumped to the conclusion that I was an unmarried missionary who had got into trouble and was escaping from China by the back door. This broke down the constraint between us and completely banished my resentment at being prevented from travelling alone.

Next morning I woke to see the dawn, and there was Jimmie with a cup of early-morning tea — a thing I have always loathed — and this was not even China tea. But I enjoyed his English breakfast of bacon and eggs, and then off we started.

Brocklehurst had asked me to stop wearing my Chinese robe and, indeed, there was no point in doing so now that I was with him, so at midday I got out a clean shirt and took my new leather waistcoat to the stream to wash and change. The sunlight was fine and warm, and so was I, but my mysterious itches were increasing. I found a little pool where I had a good wash and then I put on my clean clothes and sat down and took a good look at my old ones. As I thought, something was moving in the seams. I ran back to the camp.

"Jimmie, what are these?" I said and held out my gown.

His face lengthened and the smiles vanished, but he said nothing.

"You see something?" I went on.

He nodded.

"Are they lice?"

"Sorry, missy, yes."

I was delighted; now I was one with the great travellers. I had been bitten by rats, and had had bedbugs, fleas and lice.

Jimmie was greatly cheered by my reception of his news.

"Soon fix them with paraffin," he said, and took my lousy clothes.

All day we pushed on in beautiful weather. I bought a big oiled Chinese bamboo hat in one town and persuaded Brocklehurst to visit a lovely old temple and light incense sticks before the god of travellers. Just before sunset we camped again. After dinner I was delighted to see that after Brocklehurst had finished his nightly ritual of sharpening his knife he took out some wool and began to knit. There he sat, looking like a Red Indian in the firelight, gravely knitting the last sleeve of a sweater, "for my brother," he explained. I envied him, for I had no wool and contented myself with sharing my pipe with Jimmie.

When we arrived at Laokai, where we had to deliver the load for the lady missionaries and get new donkeys, we changed into tidy clothes and I put on a skirt before going to the mission. The two women were living in a small, poor little house, much inferior to the one in Tali. They were quite young and were obviously very pleased to see us and grateful for the load we had brought; they pressed us to come back to dinner. We arrived back in the evening for dinner and found that they had gone to enormous pains in preparing it. They could only afford part-time help so they had done most of the cooking themselves. The little room they lived and slept in was all polished and shining; the white cloth on the table almost hurt our eyes. They were a little embarrassed when they asked us to sit down and put Brocklehurst and me side-by-side on the couch.

"I hope you don't mind," one of them blurted out, "but we told the maid you were married, and married people in China always sit side-by-side at dinner."

They too had the same extraordinary blind spot I had met before. All the Chinese in the caravanserai where we were staying the night knew we were not married — the donkey-men who had come with us would have told them — so what possible good would it do to pretend they did not know?

I liked the missionaries; they were such nice girls and so keen. I asked them if they did medical work.

"No," said the eldest. "I am a trained nurse but I do not want to feel that they only take an interest in Christianity in order to get medical attention."

The dinner was a sumptuous spread, and it worried me — and Brocklehurst too — to think that they had spent so much when they had so little to spend. It is true that we had brought them a load, but even so it was very generous of them and all we could do for them was to let them talk and tell us about their work. It had been months since they had seen any other Europeans and we felt they were really enjoying it.

Next morning we made a late start. Jimmie had arranged to hire some ponies but of course everything went wrong on the first day and, while the pony argument was still raging and nothing settled, I went off on my own and rambled happily about Laokai. I wondered which I would have really enjoyed the most: being on my own or being looked after and arranged for as I was now. I knew that afterwards I would be sorry that I had not done it on my own but there was a carefree comfort about this journey that was hard to resist.

When at last I returned to the caravanserai everything was fixed up, but Brocklehurst and Jimmie showed signs of strain. We had a good Chinese lunch in the inn and then started off, and before long we were in real country, with the lovely desolation of sparsely inhabited land. We camped that night not very far from a village, and next morning as I went out to do my daily duty I noticed a thin sow wandering in a hopeful manner about the hillside. I thought nothing of it and attended to my business when I was shocked to hear the sound of running feet and ecstatic grunts. Looking over my shoulder I saw the sow with a positive smile on her face rushing down the hill towards me. The words of my host at the sewage farm flashed through my mind, as I hurriedly adjusted my clothes and prepared to run for it: "There will be pigs, then."

The days slipped by, and I could hardly remember my struggles to get onto buses, and the rat- and insect-haunted inns; I still missed my former close contact with the Chinese, though there was no doubt that this was a much easier way of travelling.

We were now coming to the best part of the journey and travelling across the country through which the Mekong and Salween cut their way. The mountains ran roughly north and south, and we were going west, so we were always going either up or down a precipitous mountainside. This was not a popular road, though I was surprised to learn that the British had built bridges across the two rivers. Why and when they built them I never discovered, but it was long before the First World War. We laboured up to the top of one of these interminable hills and looked down for the first time on a thin, lively thread of silver which was the Mekong, at least a couple of thousand feet below. I felt that even if I had enjoyed no other part of the trip, this moment would have been worthwhile.

Leaving the plodding ponies far behind, I scrambled down by all sorts of short-cuts to where the slender bridge was suspended between two once-fortified gate-houses. The English engineers had managed to make quite a Chinese-looking job of them, and the bridge was on the same model as the one we had lurched across in the lorry. It was in no better condition, so crossing it on foot was going to be quite tricky. The river ran below at a tremendous speed and gave a kind of menacing growl, though this was its quietest season; when the snow melted it would be terrifying. I must have been gazing hypnotized at it for a quarter of an hour when the ponies arrived. The poor beasts were disgusted at the idea of having to cross such a structure and the pony-men tried all kinds of lures to tempt them to cross, but they dared not blindfold them for the boards were so uneven that it was essential the ponies should be able to see where to put their feet. We unfastened their loads and carried them across the bridge ourselves, and then Brocklehurst took a hand. He went quietly up to the leading pony, which was the most intelligent, and stood beside it, stroking it and talking softly and steadily. And then, foot by foot, he coaxed it towards the bridge, talking in exactly the same tone of voice and keeping its head and neck pressed against his body until they were onto the bridge. Once it was clear that he was going to make it, the pony-men led their ponies down, and they all followed their leader without trouble. It was a beautiful sight, for I always love to see a person do something really well; and the pony-men were just as impressed as I was, and grateful too.

We spent one delightful night camping in an ancient cemetery. The tombs were round houses, with a verandah in front and a stone table outside, which was just right for our dinner. There was lovely green grass at our feet and the view was magnificent, as it so often is from rich Chinese tombs. I had not been able to bear watching Brocklehurst knitting away each night when I had nothing to do, so I had unpicked my oldest sweater and was busy knitting it up into socks. After dinner we would sit for an hour with our knitting while he told me stories about the Antarctic, or Abyssinia and his pet lions. It was a good way to end a good day.

We now had come to the dividing of the ways; we were going on the northerly road which ran north-west to Myitkyina through tribal country where some of the tribes had ferocious reputations, while the southern road — which was more used — ran south-west to Bhamo.

We crossed the Salween before we reached Tengyueh, the last town in China. The river was very different from the Mekong; it looked much wilder but without the same frightening impression of power. The bridge was much the same as the previous one, but it did not bother us now. The pony-men were very cheerful as we neared the town, for they never cared for country or camping out in the open. They much preferred to bundle up with a crowd in a caravanserai. Tengyueh itself was very beautiful, with a wall all round it, and inside it hummed like a beehive. One could feel that it was a frontier town.

Here we had our last change of animals, but no one was particularly keen to come with us. There was hardly any trade with Burma along our route, and what there was, was mostly smuggling. The smugglers did not want to come with us for they knew that once we were in Burma we would be on friendly terms with the district officers. At last we managed to pick up some ponies in a very poor state and, after a night in the caravanserai, started out in the morning.

Almost at once we seemed to be leaving China. The tiny villages we passed and all the people we met belonged to small tribes that had failed to compete with civilization and so had retreated before it.

During the first night we were sharply reminded that we still had to reckon with Chinese farmers. We had camped on a very pretty little field on a gentle slope beside a small river. All round us were high, tree-covered hills; the evening was cool enough to enjoy a fire, and after even one night in a caravanserai it was bliss to breathe the sweet-smelling air. Snug in my sleeping-bag I drifted off to sleep, planning to spend my days in a farm hewn out of the wilderness. I was woken by a ghastly feeling of cold, to find that my sleeping-bag was full of water. In the dim light I could see that we were all lying in three inches of water, and as I struggled out of my bag a volley of oaths from Brocklehurst assured me that he was just as wet as I was. In a minute Jimmie and the pony-men were awake, and a light up on the hillside showed us the cause of the trouble. The owner of our field had been irrigating it by diverting water from the river onto his land. Somehow I do not think it was an accident but a shrewd way of getting rid of us without argument, for I cannot believe that it was his custom to get up in the middle of the night to water his fields.

During the next few days we passed through the country of the Laos. We had been told that they were dangerous, but our information was very out-of-date and they proved to be friendly enough, though rather shy. If we stopped quite still and kept quiet, they would come up close and inspect us thoroughly. The Laos made lovely little bridges of bamboo over the rivers. Every now and then we would come on remains of the former tribute road, and sometimes for a few hours we would be picking our way between the jumbled flagstones that were all that was left of what had once been a paved highway with regular posting stations.

China gave us a lovely farewell. The frontier line ran along a ridge of the hills, and as we climbed up it we came to masses of raspberries — wild yellow raspberries — and so juicy that they quenched our thirst. We all separated and wandered about picking the berries, hardly noticing we had arrived at the crest of the hill. Satiated at last, I looked up and saw we were on the frontier. There was no Customs post, no soldiers, no wall or fence, but it was clearly and unmistakably the frontier. On the Chinese side the old tribute road was no longer visible — a wandering footpath and raspberry bushes were all I could see — while at my feet on the Burma side was a track, graded and ditched, wide enough for a jeep, and it led downhill through a magnificent forest. It was all so organized and so admirable, but it made my heart sink a little as I started down the path.

Also by Beryl Smeeton

THE STARS MY BLANKET

After the restrictions of an Edwardian girlhood, Beryl Smeeton cherished the freedom to travel alone, and became a globetrotter on an epic scale. Friendly and genuinely interested in the people of the countries she visited, she preferred to travel on crowded buses, in third-class train compartments and on foot. Just before the Second World War, she completed two remarkable journeys: in South America, a thousand-mile trek on horseback in the eastern foothills of the Andes, and in the Far East, a hike for several hundred miles through the hilly jungles of Burma and Siam (now Thailand). With her infectious enthusiasm and great capacity for fun, she enjoyed even the roughest of experiences — being blown right off her horse in Argentina, and fording dangerously flooded rivers in Burma.

When Beryl married Miles Smeeton, she continued her adventures, both on land and on board their famous yacht, *Tzu Hang*, with all the vitality and zest for life that show clearly on the carefree, independent trips she describes here, in her second book, with such glee.